# THE GOLDEN THREAD

## Brendan Conboy

**A true story of fear, forgiveness and faith.**

**For your journey that is yet to come.**

Published by
Yellow Dog Publishing

First published September 2015
Third Edition published May 2021

© Brendan M Conboy 2015
www.brendanconboy.co.uk
Printed and bound in Great Britain

A catalogue record for this book
is available from The British Library
ISBN: 978-1-9169000-1-1

Cover design
New Generation Art
www.newgenerationart.co.uk

# Acknowledgements

To write your life story is certainly a challenge, knowing what to put in and deciding what to leave out, dealing with the memories and the issues and struggles that come from them. This is by no means my full story, but it is a window that looks into some of what I have experienced on my journey of life. I have never been alone on this journey and I am so grateful for The Golden Thread, the hand of God in my life.

I thank God for Heather, my wife, I don't really deserve to be married to such a beautiful, kind and considerate person, but I am.

I thank my family and any others that are mentioned in this book, as without them it would be a different story.

Thanks to my proof readers and supporters: Heather, Dawn and Maura

Finally, I thank each of the people that have put a little faith in me, by supporting this publication financially. Each of the people listed on the next page has contributed through my Kickstarter campaign that I used to gain the much needed support for publishing my first ever book. They pledged various amounts from £1 to over £300. Each one of these has brought this book and the legacy that it is into existence – thank you all.

Abbie Warren,
Alisdair Longwill,
Andrew Filer,
Andy Jarrett,
Andy Morris,
Ann Cresswell,
Anne Griffiths,
Annie Watkins,
Anton Wynn,
Ash Santini,
Berith Sandgren-
Clarke,
Caro Denny,
Carol McDonald,
Cheryl Shears,
Christine Knighton,
Colin Cresswell,
Darren Weyman,
Dave Shears,
David Rose,
Dawn Salmon,
Debbie Bird,
Diane Rowe,
Fiona Parker,
Fiona Spring,
Gareth
Zimmerman,
Gavin Smith,
Grant Harman,

Jane Mann,
Janet Townsend
Jarred Price,
Jason Parker,
John Read,
John Thompson,
Jon Schofield,
Jon Trim,
Karen Burridge,
Kate Sackett,
Lucy Houghton,
Martin Pearson,
Martin Shannon,
Md Shamsudduha,
Mel Reed,
Mervyn Cave,
Mike Juggins,
Nick Burne,
Paul Newbould,
Paul Wilcox,
Phil Coysh,
Phil Jones,
Roger Spiers,
Rosemary Cave,
Rosie Richter,
Steve "Scotty" Scot,
Sarah Clifford,
Steve Woodcock,
Tracy Spiers,
Trecia Filer

In memory of Jim & Eileen Conboy
Without them I would not exist

For reasons of anonymity the names of some
people in this book have been changed

# 2021 Update – Overcoming! DON'T MISS THIS PART

It's now May 2021 and circumstances have led me to now publish the third edition of this book. It was originally written and published in 2015, yet it and the subsequent books that have since followed almost never happened. I now feel that it is important to include this story in each of my published books, which you will find listed at the back of this book.

My mum died in 2011 and while sorting through her belongings, we found the start of her own life story. It was only a few pages long, but it exposed her pain and struggles in life. It was inspirational and it planted a small seed in me. I had the idea of doing the same. That idea rolled around in my head for a couple of years, but I questioned it, "How would I find the time to write"? Life was already busy running a charity.

Then, in 2013 I shared my thought with a person that I considered to be a friend. I was hoping to receive some encouragement and reassurance that I could do this, but I didn't!

This is how the conversation went:
"I'm thinking of becoming an author".
The response somewhat surprised me, "You couldn't possibly be an author".

I respected this person's opinion so I asked, "Oh, why not"?

"Because authors write 3,600 words in an hour and you could never do that"!

It was said with such authority, such confidence and knowledge and I just accepted it! "Your right, I could never do that"! I knew that my crippled finger would always slow me down, but I now know that no disability should EVER stop anyone from following a dream. This one throwaway comment would delay my writing like a curse. God was speaking to me, leading me, but a massive barrier had just been built and it would hold me back for years.

In 2015 I stepped down from fulltime charity work and managed to free up some time. It was then that I pushed the barrier out of the way and I wrote and first published this book. It felt good to have a book published. I knew that my story could impact the lives of many and to share it was a way of glorifying God, but I still struggled to consider myself as an author, with my friend's comment still echoing in my mind, *"You could never be an author"!*

In agreement, I now found myself thinking, "Yeah, it's a one-off, a fluke, anyone can write ONE book! It doesn't make you an author"!

That then was that, decision made, I'm not an author and it's time to move on! Yet, God is patient and He had other plans, but it would take another three years before I knew exactly what He would require of me.

In 2018 my kidneys had failed so badly that I had now been on dialysis for two years. We went to a Christian summer camp festival, called, "Naturally Supernatural". It was organized by Soul Survivor and this was our third year of attending. Halfway through the week, during the loud worship time, in the throng of thousands of people, I became angry with God. I sat and I cried out aloud, "O God! What am I supposed to be doing with my life? Have you given up on me? Do you no longer have any use for me? Why have you abandoned me"?

Then, in the midst of the noise and hubbub, I heard Him! It wasn't an audible voice; it was like a brain download. Some may say that it was a thought, but it was more, it originated from a supernatural source! It was so powerful, "You still have skills and tools that I have given you! I want you to use them! I haven't finished with you yet"!

I felt the warming presence of the Holy Spirit coursing through me and I instantly knew that God had heard my cry and He had responded, but I still didn't know what it meant. Skills and tools? Did He want me to continue in youth work? He had equipped me for that role, but now it didn't seem right.

Later that week, a woman that I had never met before was praying for me. She told me that she feels that God hasn't finished with me yet. She had a picture of me walking and said, "I believe God wants you to walk with your Gospel shoes on and that you will be ready to speak the good news of the Gospel".

For a brief period, once again I found myself angry and confused. I tried to explain to her, "I have end stage kidney failure and I'm waiting for a transplant! I don't think I'll be walking far too soon"!

I was bang-out-of-order, yet she humbly apologised, "I'm sorry, I'm new to this and maybe I have it wrong"?

We both returned to our seats, but something caused me to watch where she went. She was four rows immediately behind where I was sat. Now her words were echoing around my head, just like the words from five years earlier had echoed, *"You can never be an author"!*

She had said, *"God hasn't finished with you yet"!* God had told me the same, *"I haven't finished with you yet!"* Little did I know, but this was the five year old curse being undone, I was being released! *"I have given you tools and skills…"*

My mind raced through my life, "What tools? What skills"? My racing mind stopped in my first year of knowing Jesus and instantly I knew what He was telling me. I ran back four rows to the woman that had prayed for me. "I'm sorry, I need to apologise. God spoke to me through you and I was too angry to hear or understand, but what you said was spot on. I now know that He wants me to write".

In that first year of knowing Jesus, He had given me the gift (tool) and the ability (skill) of rhyming words and I had used it to become a rap artist.

I could feel the power of the Holy Spirit already forming words in my head and I was so excited! When I went home from Naturally Supernatural, I had the idea to write some teen fiction. I had previously gathered a collection of teen fiction books, which I now intended to read, in order to gain inspiration. Now, as I pawed my way through the books, I came to an abrupt halt, as I once again heard God's voice in my heart, *"I have given you the tools and skills, now use them"!*

I left the books on the shelf, then doubt tried to have the final word. *"An author writes 3,600 words an hour"!* Was that true? I decided to Google it and discovered that most authors write 1,000 words in a day. The figure of 3,600 is how many words a copy typist can produce in an hour. I had been cursed and lied to! Now though, I knew the truth and I started to write my first novel. "Issues" was written in just over a month. Then, as soon as it was published, I felt inspired to write, "My Foundation for Life". I had used the skills and the tools, but still struggled to call myself an author (the curse was strong) – *"You can never be an author"!* The fire was fading in my heart and I didn't write anything for nearly another two years (having a transplant slowed me down). Then at the end of my transplant year of 2019, it started to snow and I was once again inspired to write my first science fiction novel. Then, when "The Invasion of the MIMICS" was eventually published, I could at last call myself an 'author'. The curse had been lifted and with it came a full-on release.

Just a month later, I published my poetry book, "Rhyme Time". Soon afterwards, I was in a prayer meeting, when these words came into my head, "ONE GOD – Many names". I instantly had the thought that I had to produce a film (yes, I also make films) with this title. As the film was being made, I also knew that God wanted me to publish a book with the title and so in November 2020 I started to meditate on the many names and titles of God (over 900 in the book). As I wrote my thoughts and life related stories, I could feel God's Holy Spirit presence growing in me. Then, after just three months and halfway through writing the book, He gave me another 'commission'.

'Commission' is the word that I like to use and I see it as **COM**e together on **MISSION** with God. This time the call was to use the 'base' writing skill that He had given me *(use the skills and tools)* – 'rhyme'.   A friend of mine had recently rewritten Psalm 23 as a rhyming poem.   I had produced a poetry book and several 'spoken word' films.  Now, I felt God speak to me again, "I gave you these tools and these skills for this time.  Work with me and write the "Psalms in Rhyme".

I write to bless others and to give God the glory and so I was obedient and did as He had commanded.  So in February 2021 I also started working on "Psalms in Rhyme" and it would take over five months before it was published.

The writing was now flowing, like a supernatural river of words.   I was an author, "I AM AN AUTHOR"!

Writing two books at the same time is quite incredible and only possible with God in the mix, but as if that wasn't enough, He also gave me my first illustrated children's book to produce, "The Land of Make Believe".  He continued to pour other poems into my mind regularly, plus He gave me the first four chapters of the sequel to, "The Invasion of the MIMICS".

Just a few negative words telling me that '*I CAN'T*' had held me back, but I had learnt. Never let ANYONE tell you that you can't do something or be something!

You can find more information on each of my other published books in the back of this book.

If you would like to bless me and support me, as I bless others and give glory to God, please visit my page: Patreon.com/BrendanConboy
Thank you.

Now, I hope that you enjoy the rest of this book and the story of how God has used me and I pray that He will do the same for you.

# Faith, Hope & Charity

I hope this blesses you.

For 26 years I have considered myself to be a visionary!

I know that my visions are God given. The Bible tells us that young men will see visions and old men will dream dreams. I do have some odd and weird dreams on occasions and these are becoming more frequent, therefore confirming that I am getting older, but I also still have visions. The visions that I have been given have become reality, but they have only come into being as a result of mission.

Mission is the practical working out, bringing about fulfilment of vision. I now realise that mission, in order to succeed, needs to be supported by "faith, hope and charity".

I have heard these three words mentioned by various people for many years, but it is only now that I am beginning to realise just how powerful a combination these three things are!

Charles Swindoll says:
*"Vision is essential for survival. It is spawned by faith, sustained by hope, sparked by imagination and strengthened by enthusiasm. It is greater than sight, deeper than a dream, broader than an idea. Vision*

*encompasses vast vistas outside the realm of the predictable, the safe, and the expected. No wonder we perish without it!"*

I am now 54 years old and have been a Christian for 28 of those years. The day that I invited Jesus into my life, it was like a switch thrown and I became a channel to be used in such a way that God had planned for my life.

The time now feels right to share my story. This book has for some time been another part of the God given vision. My hope is that it will inspire others to step out and do even greater things.

# Chapter One

### Mixed Memories

Let's start at the very beginning; it's a very good place to start. Some of you may be saying that it sounds like a line from The Sound of Music, that's because it is. I can distinctly remember visiting my grandmother's house every fortnight and listening to the songs that accompany the amazing story of the Von Trapp family and their struggles to overcome the oppression of Hitler's Nazi army. When I was eight years old I didn't really understand what oppression was, but I was old enough to sing and learn words of songs. I knew every word to each of the songs. I so looked forward to these visits and to be able to play music on a Danset record player. I didn't realise it at the time but music was to become a major part of my life.

I now recognise the power that there is in music. Music stirs up something in each of us. When we are feeling low, the right tune can lift us out of the depths of despair. When we are confused, again music and lyrics can direct and guide us, influencing our decision making. I have so often used the expression "I don't sing because I'm happy, I'm happy because I sing". This is so true, as I have witnessed the lives of young people transformed through the power of singing. Singing releases self-belief, it helps to maintain our sanity. Music has an amazing ability to carry a powerful message, something that I would realise more seriously in my twenties.

The Sound of Music however, was not my first introduction to music. I grew up with two older brothers and later a younger one came along when I was eleven years old. I can remember an occasion when we went to Severn Beach with my grandmother and my two older brothers, Mike and Chris. I was five years old and Gran gave us all some money to spend. Chris and Mike decided to club together and buy the latest Beatles song 'A Hard Day's Night'. The price was seven shillings and six pence but they only had five shillings between them. They realised that if they could influence me they could also use my buying power and together the three of us bought 'A Hard Day's Night'.

I later realised that the strength of supporting each other was very powerful and that we would need to support each other through some very dark episodes in our lives.

So let's 'start at the very beginning'. It is a good place to start. I now understand that the first eight years of any child's life are the most impressionable and the most influential. Any amount of trauma can leave deep long-lasting effects. Our earliest memories form a foundation to our development. Positive memories and experiences will in most cases result in a positive development for a child. Whereas a negative and traumatic memory could lead to disaster and, almost certainly, some level of help will be required to understand the confused feelings that will be experienced later in life.

My earliest memory was one of my dad returning from the pub on a Sunday at about three in the afternoon. Mum had kept his Sunday roast warm in the oven (no such thing as microwaves then) but it had been so long it had dried up and was not fit for consumption. I'm not sure if I had reached my fourth birthday but I clearly remember my dad's drunken anger. He was so angry that he threw the plate and contents at the lounge window, smashing the large centre pane, with the plate landing in the front garden. I don't remember what happened next but I do remember the feeling of fear. That feeling would remain with me for at least the next ten years which is how long it would take before my dad admitted that he had a drink problem. The power of any addiction can be all-consuming and alcoholism slowly and gradually took over my dad's life.

At times I will say that I didn't really have a childhood and that my childhood started when I was fifteen years old when my dad stopped drinking. In fact I did play childhood games but the big change was realising that my now constantly sober dad loved me. He had always loved me but the power of alcohol with associated anger and aggression had built up so much fear in me that I couldn't see any love.

## Silly Games

By the time I had reached my fifth birthday the family had moved from the house in Stonehouse (where I was born) to Chalford Hill. My dad had discovered this picturesque Cotswold village whilst he was laying sewer pipes and fallen in love with it. The house on Silver Street was the first of many houses that my parents bought to renovate. They were both hard workers and not afraid of a challenge. I'm sure that is where I get it from. The houses that we lived in were not fit for human habitation but my parents ignored this, believing that hard work would provide the right rewards. Looking back it is amazing to realise that they saved two houses in Chalford Hill from demolition.

As children we were expected to help as best we could with these building projects. We all learn from our parents and both myself and Chris later went into the building industry ourselves. You could say "following our father's footsteps" but not all of his steps were good ones. We also learnt how to argue and fight with each other. We learnt this through the many continuous and seemingly endless nights when we would hear my dad shouting, swearing and arguing with mum downstairs.

The fear continues to grow as you lie awake in the dark... listening ... listening... waiting... waiting... for it to end.

By the time I was twelve years old I would sleep with a knife under my pillow. I never had to use it but in my head I was prepared to, if I needed to defend myself. Dad never did attack us like that though. Mum protected us and she prayed... she prayed... for protection. She prayed for it to end.

In every school you will sadly often find a school bully. I had my first experience of being bullied at primary school. I was about eight years old and a ten year old called Peter decided to start picking on me. I don't think it was just me though, he picked on anyone he could use his strength and his power over. It didn't take long before he pushed me too far. I didn't care if he was bigger and I really didn't care if I hurt him more that he had been hurting me. That day, in that playground at the age of eight, I decided to fight back. Peter came off much worse and as far as I was aware he never bullied anyone ever again. It seemed as if he had learnt his lesson. On the other hand I had also learnt a new lesson. I had for the first time ever realised that I did have power. The power to fight back would remain in me. I became like a dormant volcano. The power and destruction and hate was bubbling away just under the surface.

My brother Chris soon realised there was a volcano inside; he would tease and antagonise me "pushing my buttons". My mum used to say "don't let him wind you up", but I had no control once eruption point was reached .

One day Chris asked me if I wanted to play a fishing game. I was eight years old and he was ten. He had a fishing rod with proper barbed hooks. "You can be the fish" he said. So I rather naively put the hook in my mouth. He didn't hesitate to give a sharp tug on the line and the hook sank in deep to my top lip. I ripped it out and Chris laughed. I didn't retaliate immediately, I cunningly planned my revenge. It was sometime afterwards that I carried out the pre-meditated act. Chris would come home from school every day and run down the garden to a large plum tree. He had tied a rope from a branch and every day he would swing on it. It hung over a pile of old wooden floorboards that had been ripped out of the old unfit-for-habitation cottage. These boards were all carefully placed so that no nails were sticking up. That is until I decided to turn them over and just to make sure that he fell on the bed of nails, I cut into the rope to ensure it would snap. The plan worked well and Chris still has the scar (he tells me) on his bottom today. The other amazing thing about that incident was that he didn't realise that it had been sabotaged and there was no retaliation... this time!  As we grew older the games and violence increased but not always towards each other.

At eleven years old I started Marling Grammar School for boys.  We had also moved to a larger house with two fields but it was even less fit to live in.  There was no water and the toilet was a bucket in the shed, which we shared with rats.

One day a group of us were playing in one of the fields.  "Playing" though is not really the right word.  We were smoking cigarettes (I started at the age of seven) and setting fire to dry grass.  This dangerous game soon turned into a very serious situation as the wind got up, the fire spread and rapidly became out of control.  We all panicked, taking our tops off to beat the flames out.  The destructive power of the wild fire struck fear in us all.  We fought that fire for what seemed like a lifetime and when it was out another fear struck... "What would dad say?"  To our amazement when dad found out he said "OK let's go and burn the rest of it"!  He wanted it done and he wasn't in the slightest angry, but he also wasn't in the slightest drunk.  If he was, I am certain that it would have been a different story.

Having two fields also meant that we could have motor bikes and we had an old Zundap which

Chris rode and I rode the BSA Bantam 125cc. Mike was old enough to ride on the road with an old Suzuki 125cc. Chris liked to show off on his bike. He would ride standing on the seat and he would pull really high wheelies. I'm not sure whether he had been winding me up or if it was just pure jealousy but one day I resorted to sabotage again. I loosened his front wheel and his seat so if he tried one of his tricks it would almost certainly result in disaster. The sight of his front wheel coming off was both funny and frightening. In a split second reality dawned. He could be seriously injured or he could survive and I could be seriously injured. He was injured and I think he gained another scar to keep the other one company that he had gained from the nail incident. To my surprise he didn't retaliate. I think he just thought that he had badly maintained his bike but he later must have realised the truth as he plotted his revenge.

Our motorbike track was a figure of eight. This consisted of a lap around the field, up a jump into the garden, around the garden, take the tight hairpin bend by the lounge window and back down the garden path to return to the field. Chris was much better at sabotage than I ever was. He decided to fix the Bantem so that the throttle would stick open; adjusting the brakes so that they didn't work properly and also loosening the handle bars. It wasn't until I wanted to slow down for the hairpin that I realised something was wrong.  I made it around the bend but at such a speed, control was easily lost.   The loosened handle bars flew off as my arm went through the lounge window.  Chris was in there watching football and he started shouting at me for interrupting the game (I think it was West Ham playing).  My elbow was now resting on the window frame and I thought, apart from a broken window, everything seemed all right.  As I lifted my arm off the frame I realised that I had been leaning on a sharp point of glass.  It had penetrated my arm by at least 50mm and I had just pulled it out.  Now basic first aid training will tell you never to remove a foreign object as it is plugging the hole.  The hole rapidly became a leak and I remember using a pillowcase as a bandage.  It was a grizzly sight and all the result of silly games.  Mum couldn't drive and dad was nowhere around and so a neighbour drove me to the local Doctor's surgery.  The Doctor laid me down and told me to bite down hard on a rolled up bandage.  He told me that it would help with the pain as he stitched me back together.  He said that I had been very lucky and that he could see the artery in my arm.  Maybe my guardian angel was watching over me.  The seven stitches were more painful than the cut.  The room must have looked like a scene from a war film or a cowboy film.

This though was the second time that I had been in this room, on the same bed, with the same

Doctor, having the same arm stitched up. A year earlier I had fallen from the scaffolding that was on the house. As I fell, a bolt ripped a gaping hole out of my armpit. This injury again just missed the artery. My guardian angel was working hard. I also started to realise that each time I had a serious injury, resulting in a visible dressing or a sling, I would get sympathetic attention. I was thirteen years old when I realised that fighting was the answer to my problems. If I won, I would be glorified and revered, if I lost and was injured I would get sympathetic attention. Either way it was a win win situation. I started to look for fights in order to meet this need, but there is a fine line between fighting and bullying and I crossed it.

The silly and dangerous games continued. Chris was given a .22 air rifle for Christmas or Birthday and he was a crack shot. On one silly game occasion, he had me pinned down behind an old apple tree. As I placed my hand on the ground to stabilise myself, I felt the sharp stinging pain of the pellet and I still have the scar on my thumb today. Weapons had now become normal! So it wasn't surprising that on one occasion when Chris had been "pushing my buttons" that I retaliated with the best weapon that I could find. He had bent over to tie his lace (I think) but it could have been he was picking up rocks to throw at me. In that split second I picked up a cast iron drain pipe. It was over a metre long and 75mm in diameter. Without even thinking I smashed it across his back. The pipe snapped in half and Chris dropped to the ground. I ran, he chased, but I don't think he caught me. That time!

How far would Chris push my buttons? He found out when I was fourteen years old. I feel this age was probably my craziest age! Chris and I had spent the afternoon at Dave Rowels' house. We had been playing cards and Chris had been cheating. He was good at cheating and then bragged about how good he was. The combination of the cheating and bragging was another wind up, another form of "button pushing". I would often react by sulking. He would notice the sulk and push even harder. The card game had long finished and I was in one of my deepest sulks. It was a bit like the calm before the storm. Chris knew this and loved seeing the storm arrive, the unpredictability of what it would look like. He wasn't expecting the hurricane. I often wonder "would he have stopped pushing if he had known what was coming"? Honestly, I don't think he would have.

We were making our way back home and had to walk through Brownshill allotments. Chris was still winding me up ... pushing ... pushing. In my mind I'm thinking, "Don't make me angry". A little bit like Doctor Banner before he turns into the Hulk. Dave Rowles was there and that may have egged me on, as an audience can often do. The point where a person passes into that uncontrollable anger is often referred to as "red mist". It is a point where anger takes over and to regain control without any form of incident is rare. The mist can be calmed with the right level of calming intervention. I know this now because I have had to calm many "red mist" situations.

One moment the brick was on the ground, the next it was in my hand. I heard my own fearsome roar as I charged towards my own brother. Stopping with the brick raised above his head, I waited for that calming intervention. It didn't come. Dave just watched, probably stunned with mouth open wide. Instead what came was the button being pushed again. "You wouldn't dare, go on I dare you?" It seemed as if time had stopped. I slammed the brick down hard. The hurricane had hit Chris in the head. Blood poured down his face from the fresh wound. Fear struck me, just before the fist that followed, one hit and the light went out in my right eye and I couldn't open it for a whole week. Fear subsided, calmness returned, we both looked a mess. Reality hit us, the concern of brotherhood returned. We both had the same thought, "What would mum say?" She had enough problems of her own; she didn't need to know the truth. Chris's blood washed off and his hair hid the wound. We made a story that I had fallen whilst playing football and an elbow had hit me in the eye. The story protected both of us, but it also protected mum from the truth. She may have suspected that it was a lie but at least she didn't know the truth about the hurricane.

Although the first eight years of a child's life are the most impressionable and influential, the adolescent years can be the scariest and the most unpredictable. Chris had started to realise this and he never pushed my buttons as hard as he did on that day ever again. My unpredictable anger found me getting involved in more fights at school. Now it didn't really bother me how old or how big a person was. I had a power in me that I could use to take control. I couldn't control the drunken arguments at home but I could take control of other kids in the school. It wasn't until later on in life that I realised that this is what is referred to as "bullying" and that was what I had become, a BULLY. I even picked on teachers; they were a new level of challenge. With a bigger audience I was going to show them all that I wasn't scared. All the time though, looking back now, I know that the rage was driven by fear.

In the 70's at Marling School, some teachers would try to exercise their authority by throwing something at you. This was usually if you were talking in class which I tended to do a lot. I decided that whatever was thrown, I would throw it back. In my head I figured that was fair. The chalk hit me, I threw it back. The board rubber just missed me; I threw it back. On one occasion instead of throwing the board rubber back, I threw the stool that I was sitting on. The teacher just told me to calm down and I did, which proved that calming intervention does work. It wasn't surprising then, that when I was fifteen I was called to a meeting with the head teacher. I'm not sure if everyone had one of these meetings, but I can still remember every word of that conversation as if it were yesterday.

"Come in Conboy and sit down."
"Yes Sir."
"What are your plans for next year?"
"Don't know Sir?"
"Well let me help you. You're not coming back here."

I didn't really want to stay on to the sixth form and I can remember being excited to be told this. Looking back now though, I feel annoyed that my choice was taken away, my power was taken away. I believe that this is now one of the underlying reasons why I empower young people to make positive choices, based on information available, using the decision-making power that is within. Little did either of us know that I would return twenty years later to actually teach a few lessons in drug education?

# Chapter Two

### Easily led

Before I go any further I just want to point out that I am not proud of any of the bad stuff that I did. I am especially ashamed of the bullying, but I will go into that later.

You will probably not be surprised to hear that I did have a few run-ins with the law and I was surprised that I was only arrested twice. Either I was very good at not getting caught or my guardian angel was watching over me again. My first arrest happened when I was just thirteen. I was just getting off the bus in the bus station after school and Nigel came up to me. We had been friends since starting Primary School and had been stealing cigarettes from his grandmother's shop since we were seven. He was with two slightly older lads that I had never met before, Malcolm and Jack.

"Hey Yob, what you up to tonight"?

I was given the name Yob as a shortened form of Yobnoc, which if you haven't worked it out is my surname spelt backwards. I now believe that if you call someone something for long enough, they will over time become what they are being called. My nickname was "Yob" and I was rapidly becoming one!

In response I answered his enquiry, "not a lot, why?"

"E's just sold his bike for £30" he says pointing at Jack, "an look what 'e's bought. Show him".

Jack opened the bag to reveal a thousand bangers (fireworks not sausages), a hundred packs with ten in each pack. Another bag contained 24 air bomb repeaters, each one with two highly-charged explosive flares.

"There's plenty to go round if you want to join us" came the invitation from Jack.

Later that dark November evening in 1973, Chalford Hill was terrorised. To us it was just a little bit of fun. We threw bangers everywhere, every garden along every street was a target, but the people that were "special targets," such as teachers, had two air bomb repeaters with a total fire power of four explosions. These lethal devices were aimed tactically at doors and windows. This was such a foolish thing to do and it is a miracle that no-one was injured. That is until PC Ted Moore caught up with us. His arrest technique was most brutal. I could see a dark figure looming behind me, torch in hand, slightly out of breath, slightly overweight.

"Don't move!" he shouted as he pushed me against a wall that was covered in a thick layer of ivy. I disappeared into the ivy and his torch came in hard, hitting me on the right cheek and splitting my face open.

"Don't move!" WHACK, "or I'll hit ya!"

No matter how many times I play it back in my head that WHACK always comes before hearing those words, "I'll hit ya". It was the early 70's and good old-fashioned policing was very effective. To be fair to Ted, he was in the process of a single- handed apprehension of four youths armed with explosives. However, by the time he caught us, the air bombs were all gone and we only had a handful of bangers left. We were all charged with contravening the Explosives Act, which sounded extremely serious but at the time was just fun.

Soon after the arrest my parents were called to Brimscombe Police Station to collect me. As soon as I saw them I said, "Dad he hit me... look!" As I pointed to the cut, the only reply that came was, "damn well serves you right! Now get in the car!"

In court we were all found guilty and I never really had much to do with Jack after that.

From about the age of 12 to 15 I took quite an interest in football. I played in goal for the 1$^{st}$ Chalford Hill Boys Brigade. Our big rivals were the Scouts and we were always guaranteed a match full of fouls on both sides.

For me, football was associated with aggression. It was the early 70's and there was an increasing problem of football hooliganism.

A group of us would catch a coach from Stroud to Swindon for every home game of the "Robins".

The acronym of "STAB" was everywhere around Swindon and you could even find it scribbled on the walls in Stroud. STAB – Swindon Town Agro Boys! I was drawn to that acronym, like a moth to a flame. My trips to Swindon were not about football, it was just another way of being able to fight, of letting off steam and putting myself at risk again. I can't recall one game of football although I was there, but I do remember chasing the away team supporters through the town on many occasions.

I dressed as if I was looking for trouble... short jeans, tall boots and braces. We had strength in numbers. The police would watch, but we were untouchable... or so it seemed.

I remember West Ham United being drawn to play Swindon in the FA Cup. It was an evening match, so probably a replay. My brother Chris is an avid West Ham supporter and as he too had been used to travelling to Swindon in the supporters' coach, he decided to travel the same way for this game. Chris and a friend of his were the only ones wearing claret and blue. They stuck out very obviously within a sea of red and white.

The journey up to Swindon was fine, but West Ham won and on the way back, the minority of claret and blue became an easy target. Small objects were being lobbed at Chris and his friend, as the hate was rising.

Suddenly a Swindon fan in front of me was jumping up and down, shouting that he was going to kill the West Ham fans (or words to that effect). He had strength in numbers and he felt safe, but something then snapped in me. My brother was being threatened! Chris could have easily looked after himself, but some form of primeval protection instinct took over and I punched the Swindon supporter in the face. The sharpened snake ring that I was wearing did what it was designed for; slicing the cheek; blood appeared instantly.

The coach stopped at Chalford and it was time to get off. Perfect timing! We quickly made our way from the coach and as it headed off, we realised that one of the ring-leaders of the aggression towards Chris and his friend also left the coach with us. Now with the odds of three to one we made sure that he would live to regret what he had started. I don't think we ever caught that coach to Swindon again.

I started to follow Liverpool FC for two reasons: One, I had a red and white scarf from following Swindon and two, the sight of the Anfield Kop End was an impressive, powerful sight and I also wanted to be associated with that power.

Liverpool was a long way to travel, but the opportunity arose for me to go to an away game at Derby County. Meeting up with Liverpool fans from Gloucester at the train station, we looked like a mini version of the Kop End. We felt powerful, nothing could stop us, the train was ours, throwing every light bulb out of the window and arming ourselves with toilet rolls for the match.

The transport police waiting at the Derby station didn't have to look very hard for someone to arrest. I was dressed for trouble and now with a British Rail toilet roll sticking out of my pocket, they grabbed me.

In a small police office, in a not-so-obvious part of the station, I denied that I had stolen the toilet roll. They told me to look closer at the toilet roll and pointed out that it had printed words on every sheet... "Property of British Rail"... I could deny it no longer! They processed me so quickly and let me go on to watch the match. As I left the room, I realised that they had many others to process and that we would all meet up together again for our day in court. I was 15 years old and it was the last football match that I ever went to. I think I may have started to learn a lesson; I may have even started to change, ever so slightly, although some of those I was with have since gone on to commit far more serious crimes. I often look back and think that I could have gone that same way, but now realise that once again my guardian angel was watching over me in that Derby train station.

I never told my parents about this latest arrest and thought that it would just go away. Then about three months later a policeman arrived at our house. By this time my dad had stopped drinking and we had moved to yet another house – a new start my parents called it.

It seemed like it was different. My dad now seemed more concerned and supportive. He accompanied me to court, back in Derby. I had the day off school. My dad liked to gamble on the horses and looking at the newspaper, I picked two horses to have a gamble on. "Village Thief" and "Head Master" were the two horses that I picked. The names seemed appropriate. Placing the bet before court and collecting my winnings afterwards, I won enough to pay my fine and I had what I regard as one of the greatest

days out with my dad.  He was there for me!  He
was supporting me!  I could see that he really did
care for me, even if he did influence me to
gamble at an early age!

### A thread of goodness
My mum's influence was a complete contrast.
Her dad, my grandfather, who had died before I
was born, was a Methodist Church Lay Reader.
His contemporaries would have referred to him
as a "true man of God".  His influence on his
daughter, my mother, was now influencing me.

A friend of mine recently told me that she had
been praying about me writing this book.  She
told me that God had shown her a picture of a
tapestry, with a silver thread running through it.
The tapestry is my life and the thread is God's
influence.  The thread ran through the whole
tapestry she told me.  I have since then grown
this picture in my own mind.  There are times,
when we look at the tapestry of our lives and
perhaps wonder where God's hand is in it, but
turn the tapestry over and there you will find the
continuous thread.  In my mind I have also
increased the value of this thread, of God's hand
in my life.  I now see this thread as a "Golden"
thread and am so thankful that God has watched
over me, since the day I was born.

Looking back now, I can clearly see that the
thread of God's influence was in the Methodist

Church Sunday School that I attended. Every Sunday I was there with my mum and two older brothers. Dad only ever went on special occasions such as the Christmas service or the annual Sunday school play (where I first started to perform). He was born and had grown up in Ireland, an Irish Catholic who had married an English Protestant.

A child doesn't understand or even care to understand about such things. What they do understand is that those times when both parents are there watching and supporting you are very special times.

I was seven years old, when one morning a new kid arrived at Sunday school. Mark Woodhouse had just moved with his mum from Plymouth. His mum became friends with my mum and the two of us started a friendship that still exists today, 46 years later.

When Mark turned up at school and was walked into the class, with Miss Poulton teaching us, he was asked if he knew anyone. He pointed at me and said. "I know him, he goes to my church." I remember thinking at the time, "actually it's MY CHURCH, I was there before you!" I now know that none of us own the Church, as we are the Church, the Body of Christ, and God's Church. As children though, we have an interesting perception.

I previously mentioned that I was a member of 1<sup>st</sup> Chalford Hill Boys Brigade. Most of the children in the village either went to Boys Brigade or Scouts. It seemed that if your parents went to church, you were more likely to attend Boys Brigade, as it was then compulsory to attend church, if you wanted to attend Boys Brigade.

Every week we would gain points for our squads for the way that our uniforms looked. We were being inspected, just like the armed forces, but if you were not in church on the previous Sunday, you instantly lost your squad ten points! This would lead to peer pressure to attend church, in order to be the top squad of the year. Although I now disagree with this incentive method, which I don't think exists any more, the Gospel seeds that were sown were many. I am now forever thinking back over a scripture and remembering that I first heard this at Sunday school or later in Bible Class.

Bible Class was a place where you didn't have to fight to prove yourself. The only fighting was in Bible searching quizzes. The friendships grew and everyone always looked forward to the annual Boys Brigade Display or Church Parades which involved a march with the band around the village. Then of course there was the annual camp. This was always at Charmouth in Dorset and always with the Girls Brigade. We were

always joined by Bath and Romsey BB & GB
and needless to say that at the end of every camp,
I always had a new girlfriend.

Momentous occasions are what help to shape
and develop us for a more positive future and it
was in 1975 (the same year that I was arrested in
Derby) when the Chalford Hill BB & GB had a
chance to perform at the Royal Albert Hall. The
day left a lasting impression and I still love it
when I have a chance to tell people that I
performed there. They are usually surprised to
hear it and even more surprised to hear that I was
dancing. Every young person that took part
formed a bond, as part of a team and we all keep
those memories.

John and Brenda Evans ran the BB & GB and
looking back, I now regard both of them as my
positive role models, my mentors and much
more.

My mum had struggled with my dad's
alcoholism for around twenty years. The
problem had slowly and gradually increased. At
times of high risk, mum would seek sanctuary
standing outside the house. She would wait until
all of the lights had gone out, wait another half
an hour or so, then slip back indoors. She now
knew though that she could not do it alone any
longer. Her love for dad had not diminished and
when you love someone, you want to do what

you can to help them. Alcoholism is a disease and diseases can be healed. Mum had been praying for around twenty years for dad to be set free from this addiction and for life to change.

Twenty years is a long time to carry the burden alone, but now mum decided it was time to share this need for prayer. Shame had prevented her until now... Pain though had become too much and she asked Brenda Evans to pray. The Bible tells us that where two or three are gathered, there He (God) is in our midst. It also says that if two of you agree about something, it will be done by our Father in Heaven (Matthew 18:18-20). Within a year of mum sharing her burden, my dad had stopped drinking.

I was fifteen years old when dad walked into Stroud Police station. He was drunk, but had also realised that he had "reached the bottom of the Pit."

He asked a young Police Constable for help and was told to go away. An older and wiser Sergeant stepped in and asked if Dad was serious. Having convinced him of his desperation, the Sergeant gave a drunken Irishman a bed (in a cell) for the night. Next morning breakfast was provided, followed by a sober conversation. That conversation led to Dad getting the help and support that he needed. The closest clinic for alcohol addiction was in

Birmingham, but with help from a sponsor that he met through Alcoholics Anonymous (AA), Dad went there and change was almost instant.

The clinic played their part, but the main work and the reason for the dramatic change was answered prayer. God had won this battle. Dad had changed, but it would be years before I would recover from the lasting, impacting effects.

# Chapter Three

### Hanging on

I will often refer to 1975, the year that my Dad stopped drinking, as the start of my childhood. It was the start of peace at home and the start of having a Dad who wasn't scary.

However, the previous year of 1974 was probably the darkest of my teenage years. It was the year that my grandmother died. She had been so reliable, always there! From the early days of "Sound of Music" to now, when I would cycle down to Stonehouse with Mark Woodhouse. She would make us egg and chips which were amazing! Was her death the tipping point? Probably not, but it was a definite contributing factor!

I was fourteen years old... impressionable... confused... angry... seeking... looking for love... looking for answers... looking for a release! SEARCHING FOR HELP!

I searched in many places. In a complete contrast to what I was being shown at church, I drifted into the occult. I was drawn to the dark power, the thought of being able to "tap into" a spiritual realm.

At church I was learning nice, interesting Bible

stories, but they weren't enough. I needed power! With power I may be able to take control of the things that I had no control over. Those things in my life that were out of control!

It started as a bit of fun. A derelict house was a perfect setting. No electricity, just one candle on a tea chest as a make shift table. A single word on each side of the table was written on a piece of paper, "Yes" on one side, "No" on the other. An upturned glass was placed in the centre and we all placed our hands on it. We asked questions but had no answers. There were at least four of us there and someone started to push the glass. We asked questions... We made up the answers. It was all a bit of fun (or so it seemed). We met regularly to conduct these "pretend" séances. Nothing ever happened and someone always pushed the glass. We all had a laugh, pretended to be scared and saw it as a bit of fun.

Finding a book of Voodoo on the shelf of the school library was a real find (I hope it's not still there). The spells and incantations were a lure to someone like me. I started to cast spells and aimed the worse one at teachers. I'm not sure if anything happened to my teachers, but my life continued to be one of fighting and bullying at school. I soon became bored of Voodoo, but little did I know that I had taken another step to expose myself to spiritual darkness. More about this shortly, but those who can remember cast your mind back to 1974.

It was the era of platform shoes and I had four inch heels with three inch platform soles. Needless to say these were some of the biggest and most dangerous. By now I was even more into music and would help out as a "Roadie" for a band. I would then dance in order to help to get the crowd going. Three times I fell off my platform shoes and three times I ended up in plaster. Now you are probably thinking that a plaster cast was a little excessive for a twisted ankle? The problem though was that, by the time I went to hospital, the injury had become more than just a twisted ankle. I suddenly realised that if I made the injury worse, the loving attention would be more. I had experienced this following my genuine accidents resulting in injury, now I could control the level of injury and as a result feel better.

I would sit on my bed at the end of an evening with a twisted ankle and wrench my foot as hard as I could. This progressed to hitting the swelling with a hammer. There was a release every time I hit. I wanted to be released and now I had found an exit for the pain in my life. By creating a more intense temporary pain, the other constant pain and fears seemed to subside. At last I was in control of something. When I was bullying other people, I was taking control, but this behaviour always resulted in trouble for me.

Now, I could channel my anger, my fears and anxieties on myself.

I carried on injuring myself in this way until I was about seventeen years old. Every small accidental injury was transformed into a more serious injury. No matter whether I had an arm in a sling or a leg in plaster, I was always able to tell a story of how it happened. Though it wasn't until I was thirty seven years old that I realised what I had been doing is referred to as self-harm and I had done this. To me, I just knew it as FREEDOM!

I often wonder did I go down the road of self-harming because of my involvement in occult practices. Quite possibly!

It was the summer of 1974 when I met up with some girls from BB and GB summer camp. They lived in a house with an attic room and it seemed the perfect setting for another "pretend séance". By now I was well practised and familiar with the process and knew it would be fun. I also knew that it would be a little exciting for the two girls who had never done it before. How wrong I was!

The room was cluttered with old furniture. Dust lay on every surface. It looked spooky. I sat opposite a wardrobe with a full length mirror. The girls sat either side. The usual items were laid out on the table. I was already thinking, "This situation shouldn't be any different to the previous times. I'll just push the glass and frighten the girls a little, it'll be fun". At least that's what I thought.

I now believe that each of the previous times and the combination of voodoo had lowered my resistance and made me vulnerable. This time was different! Almost immediately after asking the first question, "Is there anyone there?" an apparition of an old lady, all grey looking, appeared in the mirror opposite me. I panicked, I freaked out, wanting to hide. This was suddenly scary, now it was real! The figure disappeared almost as quickly as it had appeared, but where had it gone? It would be another fourteen years before I would find out the answer to that. I decided that was the last time I would touch anything to do with the occult. However, horoscope remained a daily, innocent topping up. I didn't understand or realise that this too is linked to the darkness of the occult.

### More silly games
My friendship with Mark Woodhouse had by now grown over seven years. His mum had told my mum once that they had called him "Mark" because it couldn't be shortened. Of course we all saw this as a challenge and thought, "No it can't be shortened, but it can be changed." The Methodist hymn book had a composer of hymns

in it called "Percy Dreamer". Mark did seem to be a bit of a "Dreamer" so we decided to call him "Percy".

During the long boring summer holidays of 1974 we borrowed our mother's twelve inch carving knives and headed to the playing field. The game was "Chicken", throwing the knife at your opponent to see how close you could get without hitting him. This soon progressed to cutting some hazel branches and fashioning a bow each. A short piece of string completed the weapon, whilst the thinner, straight hazel growing at the bottom of the tree made perfect arrows. Finally sharpening the arrow tips with the knives, we were ready to do battle.

I remember the game took on a Robin of Sherwood type of theme. Percy was the Sheriff of Nottingham and I was Robin Hood. Fantasy was taking over. The role-play became real. Percy ran to the sanctuary of the tall slide. There were less health and safety restrictions then and the cage at the top of the steps was some twenty feet in the air.

"You'll never get me up here", shouted Percy from his fantasy castle.

Waiting my moment and taking my aim, I didn't hesitate, I didn't think, instincts took over and I released the arrow. The sharpened point found the soft penetrable target of the cheek. The arrow was embedded, protruding from Percy's face. The game was over, Robin Hood had won again as he always does.

Percy just pulled the arrow out, went home and put a plaster on the wound. He probably told a story to his mum that he had cut himself shaving. We had all started shaving at the age of 14 and none of us were very good at it.

This had been a dangerous game. I could have hit his eye. It could have killed him.

Interestingly years later, when I met up with Mark after being out of touch for years, he could not even remember the incident. What was even more interesting was that my friend had now become the Reverend Mark Woodhouse. The most incredible thing though was the fact that there was no visible scar.

### Pushed to the edge

By the autumn of '74 I had discovered Minchinhampton Youth Club. A group of us would catch the bus from Chalford Hill down to Brimscombe, and then catch another back up the hill on the other side of the valley to what had become known as the best Youth Club to hang out at. Disco nights would see over 200 young people and the atmosphere was incredible.

Under the lights of the disco and with a bit of alcohol, every girl looked attractive. At the end of the evening arrangements would be made to meet up again with the girl that you had met on the following Sunday afternoon. This was the pattern of trying to find the love that seemed to be missing in my life.

So, often I would meet girls on a Sunday afternoon and in the reality of day with a sober mind I would realise that it was a mistake! That was however until one particular girl who seemed different. She seemed special. Was she what I was looking for? I had been seeing her for about six weeks. This was the longest I had ever stayed with one girlfriend; was this love?

I had even started walking the long trek from Chalford Hill to Minchinhampton, a distance of about two and a half miles each way down into the valley and back up the other side. I did the journey about three or four times each week, but she seemed worth it.

Previously I had broken off with many girlfriends and some had broken off with me. The decision had been ours and I was okay with that. As I mentioned earlier, I am a great believer in allowing people choices and letting them make their own informed, educated decisions. Now, long before the head teacher decided that I was not good enough for his school, someone else was about to make a decision that would make a greater impact, more than anything else had done before now.

We were now in the dark evenings of October 1974 and I arrived at my girlfriend's house, but something immediately felt different. She wouldn't let me in! She told me that her dad had found out who she was going out with. Her dad knew my dad and he had made the decision... I wasn't good enough for his daughter.

The rejection... the hurt... the pain... the confusion...the embarrassment... the hate... the tears... the anger... the overwhelming surge of emotions... they all hit with catastrophic impact. I was already beating myself up with a hammer. Hospital had become my sanctuary, the place where I knew help could be found.

This time though, the pain was at a new level, the feeling of being out of control was overpowering, and the desire to live left me in an instant. I turned away from the doorstep and within seconds I had made my plan. The train ran through the valley every hour. I would be down there and dead within two hours. Everything was happening so fast. Decision made! I was back in control. I would make the ultimate and final decision in my life. Nothing could stop me. Rage had taken over again, only this time it was inward. This would be the end.

Rain and tears mixed on my cheeks. In the wet dark October night, no one was around to see me. No one would care. Although that Golden Thread, the hand of God is still in our lives, even when we can't see or feel it.

I had made my plans and walked two hundred metres from the doorstep where it seemed life had already ended. The light from the red phone box gave an attractive glow. I was drawn to that light shining in the darkness, on that cold wet October night. A sign next to the phone read, "Suicide, Lonely, Despair? Contact the Samaritans". The number was free to dial. I had nothing to lose.

I talked to someone who called themselves Peter. I can't remember what was said, I just talked and he listened. He made me feel valued. The desire to live returned almost as quickly as it had left. I left the phone box where I had found a new hope and walked past the train line, home to the warmth of my bed.

I am alive today because of the Samaritans. I am alive because someone took the time to listen. It didn't take long, but that phone call had saved my life.

I sum up this chapter simply by saying that I now realise that suicide is a "permanent end to a temporary problem!" My dad and his addiction was the root of my problem, but less than a year after the call to the Samaritans, my dad had stopped drinking.

Later on in life I would look back at this incident and picture it as me standing on the edge of a cliff. In my imaginary picture there is a fence. That fence is there to protect. I had been driven beyond the fence to the edge of oblivion, but then came back. However, I would also find myself back at the edge of that imaginary cliff later on in life.

# Chapter Four

### Love is a Roller-Coaster

Another friend that I grew up with was Tomo. I can recall the time that I had gone to his house straight from school. I was about eight years old. It hadn't occurred to me that I should tell my parents. I can't remember the exact time that I did arrive back home, but I do remember the rage of my dad. His patience had totally expired and grabbing me by the ear, he dragged me up the stairs, threw me on the bed and gave me several whacks with his leather belt. This whole scenario did teach me how important it is to tell your parents where you are, but I also learnt more about temper, aggression and the effectiveness of weapons.

I was now 15 years old and I had become close friends with Percy and Tomo. This may have been partly because Percy's birthday was exactly a week after mine and Tomo's was a week later. I was the oldest of the trio.

1976 was the year when my life would start to change. My dad had already stopped drinking, but now Percy and Tomo arrived with an exciting new discovery. They had travelled to Brownshill, the next village and met some girls.

"Do you fancy coming over to Brownshill?"

"What for?"

"Girls, three of them and there's only two of us. We need a third person, so one isn't left out."

With everything to gain and nothing to lose, we walked the nearly mile long journey. Brownshill bus shelter was the agreed rendezvous point and we arrived first. Shortly afterwards the girls arrived. I never was quite sure who Tomo and Percy had identified as "theirs" or "the one that I fancy," I didn't ask.

I rapidly assessed the choices, number one? No. Number two? I don't think so and number three? YES. Little did I realise how important that choice would turn out to be. The decision was so quick that I could have just been selecting my favourite chocolate bar out of a choice of three.

It is said that beauty is in the eye of the beholder and it was as if my mind said, "Behold this beauty."

The other two seemed slightly disgruntled, although by the end of the afternoon we were three couples and I had no doubt, I was absolutely certain, I had made the right choice.

I was nearly sixteen years old and Heather was only twelve. Her friends all told her that she was crazy to associate with me. My reputation was not a good one. I had a history of violence but that, I am glad to say, did not deter her.

We quickly found out that we had so much in common, yet we were also so different.

The feelings that I was now feeling were all new to me. I had never felt like this in the presence of any other girl. Something happened deep inside of me every time I met her. I began to wonder, "Is this what love is?" Having never really loved and struggling to recognise if I had ever been loved, the feeling was new, it was alien, but it felt good.

With so many insecurities though, could anything last? A tumble weed never puts down any roots and I had been tumbling through life, never entirely seeing the good things that life had to offer.

I passed my 16th birthday and I had been with Heather for six weeks. This was my longest relationship ever with a girl, but temptations were looming. I was now able to access the money that my grandmother had left me when she died and I decided to buy a moped. With a faster form of transport came a new found freedom and it wasn't long before doubt crept in... "Do you really love her?" Temptation won the battle and at the start of the summer of '76 we went our separate ways.

It took less than a month for me to realise what an idiot I had been, what I had thrown away, but it was too late. Temptation had won the first battle and now pride was continuing the fight. That fight would continue throughout the summer and beyond, nearly six months would pass before we would reunite. The summer that would pass first would be long and crazy.

With no job and no school to attend, the summer became one long alcohol-fuelled party. Some older friends were left at home whilst their parents went away on holiday and the house parties started.

First Percy's mum went away for a couple of weeks and we had the freedom to do what we wanted. Each night we would drink several cans of cheap beer and stack the empties in a triangle against the wall. Before long the triangle touched the ceiling and covered half of the wall. That was a lot of cans, especially for a bunch of sixteen year olds. Off licenses and pub landlords seemed to ignore the law and we were served in any pub that we walked into. If we didn't have a house to go to, we would just hang out each evening in a local pub beer garden, drinking and laughing.

One of the craziest parties during this time saw me stay at Nathan's house for best part of the week. At the height of the party at the weekend, the house was packed. Nathan didn't know half of the party goers.

People were beginning to act more foolishly. Inhibitions had flown away and dares were being dished out. They started small and innocent such as "I dare you to drink this" it was usually a mixture of everything going. Gradually the dares became bigger, riskier and more illegal until someone said, "I dare you to drive Nathan's dad's van!" This was the last dare of the night.

Before anyone knew what was going on, someone had found the keys and had now stormed out of the driveway. Nathan panicked... we all panicked! "Who had taken the van?" Noone knew him.

Tom grabbed his crash helmet and jumping onto his 250cc Kawazaki, headed off hastily in pursuit. People were shouting at him, escalating the confusion as he approached the fork in the road at the small green. At the last moment he realised that the onlookers were telling him that he was going the wrong way. The change of direction though came too late and hitting the kerb, Tom was thrown from the roaring motorcycle.

The danger and severity of the situation was increasing rapidly and out of control. Alcohol was the reason for the accident, in which Tom escaped unharmed, but the crowd who were also fuelled by alcohol immediately blamed the unknown joy rider of the van.

It was less than five minutes before the van suddenly returned undamaged and the driver just came out of it smiling. His smug look was saying, "there you are everyone, I did it," but it disappeared in an instant.

The alcohol-fuelled crowd had already passed the sentence and the joy rider was guilty, he had crossed the line! The sentence it seemed, had also been decided as someone shouted, "hang him" a rope appeared as if from nowhere.

The frightening reality of what was now an incident way out of control was sobering. Something prompted me that what was about to happen needed to stop. Yes, this unknown person had done wrong, but if the roller-coaster ride of events didn't stop, he could die.

God's Golden Thread that is running through my life suddenly surfaced again, as I was the first to speak out against what was in progress. Nathan agreed with me that the prisoner should be released.

The party crowd quickly dispersed but the party continued for a few more days with just a handful of Nathan's friends.

## Seek and you shall find
(Matthew 7:7)

The Bible tells us that if we have lost something, we should go out and find it. This next section is all about trying to retrieve the most valuable thing that I had ever thrown away... my relationship with Heather.

Every so often Percy and I would take a ride over to Brownshill on our mopeds. At times when my moped wasn't working, I would ride on the back of Percy's moped illegally. Riding up into the playing field, we would terrorise the younger children. All of the time, I would be looking out for Heather. Where was she? What was she doing? Who was she with?

The summer came to an end and with it some of the craziness. As I started my apprenticeship I settled down to train as an engineer... my first job. I had struggled to learn in school... too many other issues to fill my mind, but now I was learning. Life at home was happier... I was happier... my thinking was changing... perhaps I was growing up?

It had been some five or six months and my mind had changed, but I had never stopped thinking about Heather. I decided to track her down on a Saturday afternoon at the end of October or start of November. She seemed pleased to see me and told me that I could go with her later that evening as she had made arrangements to go baby-sitting. What she had forgotten to tell me was that she was now going out with an older lad. To make matters worse, our paths had crossed when we were younger. We had fought and I had suffered from his beating.

Any cares and concerns soon disappeared, as I was now with Heather. We soon settled into the cosy warmth of the small cottage with the wood burning stove casting a romantic glow around the room.

The knock at the door startled us and Heather went to see who it was. I could hear Ian demanding to come in. Heather was telling him to go away. I recognised his voice as I listened from behind the door. I waited less than a minute, but it seemed like hours. I had to fight for the girl that I hadn't stopped thinking about for months. Ian was much bigger than me though and had already proven that he could beat me in a fight. The odds were stacked against me. In my mind I had learnt that weapons were made to improve the odds.

I approached the door where the argument was taking place. Making sure that Ian could see the knife, I simply said, "she's with me, now go away!" He responded as I had hoped I am glad to say, but it could have been a completely different story and what did Heather think? What was she taking on? Would she calm the anger of the beast within?

So much had happened in the months that we had been apart, but the most important thing was that I had realised that I didn't want to lose this girl. Now thirty seven years later I am still with her, married and even more in love with her. I am so glad that I went in search of that which I had lost!

# Chapter Five

### Leaving school

The shock of being told that I was no longer welcome at Marling school had motivated me, in a strange kind of way. I remember being in an interview with a Careers Advisor.

"What do you like doing?" came the one probing question.

"Messing around with engines," was my short answer. I didn't think about it, it just came out. I had been playing around with motorbikes for at least four years.

"Engines? Then you would be good as an engineer!"

Looking back I now consider this as bad guidance. I was misled and not given any choices. I think that I really wanted to be a mechanic, but I was given a list of different engineering companies to apply to. There were thirteen in total and I wrote to all of them. Surprisingly twelve of them offered me an apprenticeship and I chose the closest one to home. Benson's International was also where my mum and dad both now worked, but it was where I would be "imprisoned" for the next four years.

I never really enjoyed the engineering industry,

but what it did teach me was attention to detail and the importance of accuracy. I carried those skills on in all areas of my life and I always tell people that no experience is ever wasted!

In the same way that I would fall off of my platform shoes and then enhance my injuries, I would now do the same at work. A slip of a spanner would result in a bruised and swollen knuckle. The accident would be immediately followed by a trip to the toilet. The spanner would be in pocket and several more whacks with that spanner would ensure that I had an injury that was serious enough for me to visit the First Aider, often then to be sent once again to hospital. My mum would joke about how I was accident prone and my hospital file was getting bigger all of the time, but every injury had a legitimate reason, an excuse; it had been an accident.

My apprenticeship involved attending Stroud College and surprisingly, I never had one physical fight whilst I was there. The inward aggression towards myself though continued, with regular visits to hospital with my self-inflicted painful wounds. I was in control of this; I controlled the pain, unlike the deeper emotional scars that had compounded over the years of childhood. My dad had stopped drinking and was now what I later learnt in life was referred to as a recovering addict, but I was also on a road to recovery.

It has been said that, "behind every great man, there has to be a great woman." Now looking back, I believe that some of what I have achieved could be regarded as "great", but I could not have done anything by myself!

My strong belief in giving people choices was given another foundation stone on an occasion when Heather said to me, "I don't like you smoking, it stinks, in fact I hate it!" Although she didn't actually say it, to me it sounded as if she was saying, "it's your choice, smoking or me." So at the age of seventeen years old I quit smoking. I had tried to stop on so many occasions, but never before had such incentive. Interestingly, it was around the same time that I stopped harming myself. I now believe that smoking is just another form of self-harm and that by stopping the one, the other left me as well. The choice to stop smoking had empowered me to stop purposely putting myself in hospital. One small choice had impacted other areas of my life...but I also believe the power of God's Golden Thread was also influencing my life again!

### Committing to more

We all need to feel security in life and by the time I was twenty years old, I had known Heather for nearly five years. My apprenticeship was ending and my parents had been offered redundancy payments at work. They were leaving Bensons and planning to start life afresh. Their plans were tempting me away from the "prison-like" factory. Their decision was a big step though. With their redundancy payment they wanted to make a new start in Cornwall. They planned to buy a small farm, but where would that leave me? Where would it leave Heather?

It was decision time again....

Choice number one – I stay here and try to find somewhere to live, but I couldn't really afford that, especially if I was escaping Benson's "Prison."

Choice number two – we just split up and go our separate ways. We didn't even consider that... we had been together for so long and were already engaged.

Choice number three – Heather comes to Cornwall and we all live on the farm. We both liked this choice, but it was a long way, a big step. It meant Heather leaving her job and family, but how much security would she have? I had demonstrated my commitment, my loyalty and gave her the security that she needed. She was only seventeen years old and I was twenty, yet we both instinctively knew that we should be married.

We married with just over three months to plan for it. I wore an old suit with a shirt that didn't fit and a pair of shoes that my brother had thrown in the bin. Heather's mum made her dress and she looked beautiful. We married on 17th January in 1981 and four days later were on our way to Cornwall.

People will often say that getting married, moving house and buying a car are some of the most stressful things in life. I made all three of these in one week, as I also bought Chris's car from him.

We made so many big decisions in such a short space of time, yet there was no stress. It all felt perfect.

This decision-making and step-taking process, I would later in life hear referred to as "taking a step of faith!" This is something that I have now done so many times. It is now an intrinsic part of my makeup and the whole process of getting married had helped to build this in me. Looking back it is easy to see where God had his hand on us both in our decision making. We didn't even know him then, but he was guiding us, with his continuing Golden Thread!

Our first home was a mobile home on the farm. It was like being on holiday and without any work, it really was a holiday or even a honeymoon.

We lived in Cornwall for exactly a year and in that time I had six weeks employment in a factory. I hated it, but it was what I knew. I also did a disco with my brother Mike. We had brought our mobile disco down with us to Cornwall, having been running this previously in Gloucestershire. Prior to disco and being a DJ, we had been in various bands, but there were always too many arguments. I had been the drummer but the drums had been sold to buy disco equipment. This was now helping to bring in a little extra income, but it was never enough.

A visit back to Stroud for the weekend made us realise what we had given up. We didn't have to think about it for long, as we stood on Rodborough Common we both said, " Isn't this view beautiful? Let's move back!"

We were amazed to find out that there was a grant available for skilled engineers that wanted to move to Gloucestershire. The county had a shortage and this was a government initiative to boost the labour force. It didn't matter that I had only left a year ago and I quickly found myself working in the factory where my mum and dad had met. RHP Ltd. was not just another factory, it was yet another "prison."

We used the £1,000 grant for a deposit on our first house and following my parents' footsteps, we bought a house that was unfit for human habitation. This was the start of my building career and I started to fall in love with this new trade.

I would start my day with work in the factory at 7.00am until 4.00pm and then go straight to my night job of house renovation. What I hadn't learned from watching my dad, I learnt from reading books. My working day would end around 10.00pm. Fifteen hours of work followed by seven hours of sleep.

We lived with Heather's step dad, Roger, where she had grown up in Brownshill. That was until Roger decided to move to Stroud and we moved with him. Our house was being completely gutted and we were technically homeless but Roger gave us a roof over our heads, whilst we kept him company.

We moved into our new home in September 1982, making it the third time that we had moved house in less than a year. At last we had security! Our own house, with good money coming in, but how long would it last?

Two months later I was called into the office at work. I was told that I was being made redundant and that I was no longer needed. I had only been there for ten months, but the sum of money that they gave me to be rid of me was enough to set myself up in business. I could now break out of this prison and do something that I now loved doing. I could become a builder. As my foreman gave me the news he looked confused. He had expected me to be disappointed, but instead I was overjoyed. I was FREE!

My redundancy money was used to buy equipment and at the start of November 1982 I was a builder, self employed and no longer with the security of regular income. Was this another step of faith? Was this another twist of the Golden Thread? I would now have less than a year before God's hand would reach out and seriously touch my life, but I still wouldn't recognise him!

I had been self employed when Heather told me that she was pregnant. We had been trying for this since getting married and despite the fact that work wasn't always secure, plus we would now have another mouth to feed, we were once again overjoyed. Life couldn't get any better! I had my own house, my own business and now I was going to be a dad! I had made it! What more could anyone want? Everything was perfect!

# Chapter Six

### A wake-up call

I was twenty two years old, my own boss and first child on the way. There were some weeks when work had been short and not much money coming in, but that would give me freedom to do whatever I wanted to do. We always had enough to get by, even though on some weeks we did only just get by.

Now as the summer approached, the work was increasing. I was glad to be given a job on the busy London Road running through Thrupp. A three storey house was in great need of some tender loving care. Heather's auntie had recently moved in and the first job on the list was the dormer windows, almost thirty feet above the ground. The paint had almost completely peeled off over at least ten years of neglect and deterioration due to weather. This was my opportunity to restore them and for them to stand out as the best in the terrace. This one job could lead to me doing the whole row! This was my lucky break, the moment had come.

The tower scaffolding was a very cheap, thin tube construction. It didn't have any adjustable feet, but the hire company assured me that it would be fine at a height of thirty feet.

With no adjustable feet and uneven ground, I needed to place some blocks flat on the ground and level up the base with appropriate sized pieces of wood.

The height didn't bother me I had been on scaffolding when I was just a child. Now I was king of my own castle, I was on top of the world.

The paintwork scraped off easily and I moved onto the process of sanding. I knew that a good paint finish required good preparation; the attention to detail was in me from my engineering apprenticeship. My mind was now focused on the detail of the work, the job in hand, so much so that other detail was being missed.

The scaffolding was wobbling! If you have ever laid a rope or a hosepipe on the ground and lifted one end up and down fast, you will have seen the movement transferred along it until it reaches the other end. My physics teacher probably gave this process a name? Now, as the energy of movement was transferring through the feeble tower, the movement at the top was being mirrored at the bottom. Every small fraction of swaying on my small platform resulted in the base being gradually walked off the makeshift packing.

That moment when the scaffolding actually

toppled was another moment when it seemed that time had stopped. I had experienced it briefly in the allotments with a brick in my hand, ready to smash into my brother's head. This time, at the start of the moment in time, a thought hit me. I am going to die! I had heard about people seeing their lives flash before their eyes, now I was experiencing it. I pictured Heather, pregnant, and imagined a child that I would never see! I pictured my parents, both still alive and I was about to die before them! I pictured my house and pictured Heather again! The pictures do just flash by. From the thought of "I am going to die," flash, flash, flash and at the end of the flashes another thought, "I want to live."

I remember my hand reaching out to the sky. Everything seemed to be happening in slow motion. FLASH....... FLASH........ I had grabbed the plastic guttering.... FLASH.... but that had given way from my weight. Why did everything seem so slow..... FLASH......?

By now the feeble frame of the tower scaffolding had completely buckled. A twisted hazardous mess of deadly steel, 30 feet below and my body was going to be reunited with it any second.... any second.... time seemed slow. My hand was reaching out to the sky. There was nothing to grab hold of, although it felt as if something had hold of me. Slowly, slowly I fell.

I landed and my back slumped across one of the steel tubes. Slightly winded, slightly dazed, I looked back up amazed. I was alive!

A pot of paint had landed in the busy road and a passing motorist had now stopped. He picked up the paint and cleared the damaged scaffolding. I watched in a daze, still in disbelief at what had just happened. The "Good Samaritan" now helped me into his car, turned it around and drove me a couple of miles to Stroud Hospital. Here I was again, only this time it was a genuine accident and I didn't like it.

The motorist left me in safe hands. I never did find out who he was, was he an angel? I don't think so, but I do now believe that my "Guardian Angel" lowered me to safety. Yes I was hurt, but nothing too serious. This I now believe was my first encounter with an angel, but it wouldn't be the last.

On admission to hospital the staff took my clothes and dressed me in an open back gown. What could they see that I couldn't? I felt fine and after a few hours I told them that I wanted to go home. This visit to the hospital was out of my control and I didn't like it. I signed myself out! I must have looked so stubborn and so ungrateful for their help, but I didn't need it, I didn't ask for it and all that I wanted was to be at home.

The next day I decided to take the day off work and think about what had happened. The lawn needed cutting and the sun was shining. As usual I stripped to the waist and took to the task in hand forgetting about the previous day.

It wasn't long before my neighbour leaned over the fence and asked if I was OK. "I'm fine," I told him, "why do ask?" He just pointed at my back and said, "you're all black." I went inside and looked in the mirror. Sure enough my back was as black as ink, yet I was in no pain. I could have and probably should have broken my back, but instead all I had was one huge black mass that covered my whole back.

### Fear creeps in

Never wanting to allow a task to beat me, I went back to the dormer windows, but this time I contracted a professional scaffolding company. I figured that I had learnt the hard way on this job and now the profit had gone. I did finish the job, but failed to make any money! To make matters worse, no more work came in. Perhaps the news of my fall had put people off using me?

A while later, my brother-in-law Eric asked me to help him with some work on his roof. He had recently bought his house and as I climbed up onto the roof ladder, to re-bed the ridge tiles, I started to shake.

Panic and fear came into my mind, rapidly taking over my thoughts. Flashbacks, the mind plays tricks, with memories of the fall that I had recently taken. I could barely do the work and Eric could see it. Heather was pregnant and I was going to be a dad in just a few months. Eric reminded me of this.

"You shouldn't be doing this kind of work now with a kid on the way; you need to keep your feet on the ground!"

I didn't argue with him, fear had a grip of me. As I returned to the solid concrete path below, the fear left me and calmness returned. It was a little like sea sickness. When you are out at sea and you are ill, you just want it to end. Then when the boat returns to shore and you set feet on solid ground, all of the motion sickness leaves and normality returns.

I talked to Heather about the lack of work and consequently the shortage of money. I never did tell her about the fear that gripped me on Eric's roof.

Things became so bad that we didn't have any money to put food on the table. If this happened today we would be able to receive charitable hand-outs from organisations like Food Bank, but there was nothing like that! We had to work this problem out for ourselves. I can remember saying, "if we can't put food on the table, what's the point in having a table?"

We decided to sell the table and the money fed us for over two weeks, but what about when it would run out? There was no other option, I would have to go back to what I was qualified to do; I would have to go back to engineering.

I wasn't keen to return to the prison of the factory, but I knew it had to be done. Any job was better than no job at all. My building career had come to an abrupt ending. I had failed in business. I felt REJECTED!

I have always had the ability to sell and this time, reaching for the telephone, I was trying to sell myself. I didn't stop. I called one number after another. I was determined! Soon there would be another mouth to feed. I know that motivation and determination will always pay off and by the end of the day I was offered a job. I had lost count of the number of phone calls I had made, but I had succeeded. I would now have a steady income. We would be able to pay the bills and put food on the table. We would have to buy a table again at some point though.

It has been said that we learn from our experiences and especially our mistakes. This would not be the last time though that lack of finance would become my enemy.

# Chapter Seven

## New beginnings

Springfield Engineering seemed different. This was not a big firm, but they were growing. They had allowed me to become part of that growth. There was a great atmosphere and friendships within the workforce. The relationships were fun and we enjoyed each other's company. Each day we would laugh together, but it was still engineering. Locked up! I missed my freedom.

It was November 1983 and our son Chris was born. Suddenly, becoming a dad made me think a little about the miracle of creation. Questions started to come to mind such as, "What is life all about? Why are we all here? Where does God fit into the equation?" Becoming a parent had thrown a switch in my mind. The thoughts and the questions were looking for answers, but I didn't know where to look for them!

With a regular income and a family, we decided that we should move to a bigger house, but finding the right house proved to be harder than we had imagined. We went for one house after another, only to lose out to someone else. The house that we eventually moved to was our fourth choice. It almost felt as if we were led there, guided by some unseen force. Interestingly, we have moved four more times since and each time we were guided by that same unseen force. Nowadays that force has a name, but right then we didn't recognise him.

The house was a more modern design. There wasn't much room to improve it. We weren't going to climb many steps up the ladder with this one. Why were we here?

The neighbours were very friendly on one side. They introduced themselves as Kim and Paula Brown. They were about the same age as us and had a son about the same age as our son Chris. Kim had also been a DJ and had a similar record collection to mine, all labelled and indexed in a manner that any song could be found within seconds. This was going to be an inevitable friendship.

It was a few months later that a lady living a few doors up the hill, stopped me in the street and commented, "You live next to Kim and Paula Brown, don't you?"

She seemed friendly enough so I answered, "Yes, do you know them?" I've always liked answering a question with a question, it's the art of conversation.

"Yes, I know them," she answered, "but they're a bit weird!"

"What do you mean, 'weird'?" The tone of the conversation was changing. She seemed to be on the attack, wanting to find fault in our apparently perfect neighbours. "Weird? In what way are they weird?" I asked almost in defence.

"They call themselves 'Born Again Christians'!"

The conversation ended and I can remember walking home and thinking, "is that really weird or is it really interesting?"

Kim and Paula were very interesting and we would watch them from a bedroom window, particularly on a Sunday morning. At times they would leave long before 10.00am and often not return until mid afternoon. What sort of church were they going to? We were inquisitive, intrigued, more questions... where were the answers?

Having moved and been given a new mortgage, it seemed a perfect time to consider another career move. I missed the freedom of being my own boss, but didn't want to return to building work.

An advertisement in the local newspaper caught my eye. It was intriguing in the sense that it didn't really say what the job was. I expected that it was some form of sales work. It said that I could earn loads of money, no experience was needed and all training would be provided. It talked about fast-track promotion and other temptations. I made a phone call and was offered an interview almost immediately.

The office was a new environment for me. The old wedding suit came out for the first time in three years. The interviewer was only a few years older than me. It was September 1984 and I was offered the job as a "Financial Consultant", which was just a fancy title for Life Insurance Sales Person.

I would be in this role for the next eighteen months and would do exactly as the advertisement had said. I would become fast-tracked to become a manager with my own sales team. I would become a top sales person and find myself listed in the top ten sales consultants for the company. I would rise high, only to be dropped, but before the drop I would interview someone for a job. That interview and that 'person' would change the course of my life!

For now though, for eighteen months, I immersed myself in my new career. Every day was spent in the office in Bristol making appointments and most evenings would be out visiting those appointments. I would leave the house around 7.30am and work until at least 9.00pm. The pay was commission-based, which translated in my mind as effort related. If I didn't earn enough one month, I would aim to bounce back the next month and make up for it.

Our second child was born during this working period, in December 1985. Ellie was a beautiful looking baby, but after her birth I had hardly stopped to notice. I now always look back and feel that I missed most of the first year of her life. Work had taken over and if I stopped for too long, the money would also stop. Here we were again with financial insecurities, no regular income, the only way to increase our security it seemed, was to work harder and harder.

I did find time to relax at weekends and we would often find ourselves chatting to Kim and Paula next door. Eventually we were invited round to their house for a meal. Lasagne and salad was dished up, followed by a dessert that I can't remember (probably Lemon Meringue). At the end of the meal we sat drinking coffee and chatting. Until now we had never talked to Kim and Paula about what the lady up the road had told me. Likewise, they had never pushed their beliefs onto us. Now as we sat relaxed I asked a question. At the time it must have seemed as if it had come from nowhere. However, later we realised that my question was an answer to prayer. Kim and Paula had been praying for us since the day that we had moved in.

Now I asked the question, "I'm really interested

in something," I started tentatively. I didn't want to upset them, but I was puzzled. "We just ate a meal and neither of you said Grace beforehand, yet we have been told that you are something called 'Born Again Christians'?"

They both explained that they didn't want to offend us, so had both just prayed in their heads. That one question led to question after question. The conversation lasted about three hours, ending in the early hours of the morning. This couple had something special. The detail of the conversation has long been forgotten, but the feeling of hearing the truth of the Gospel was exciting. This pair were talking about things that I had heard at Boys Brigade and Bible Class, but this time it was more than just a story. It was real and it was alive in them.

By March 1986 we'd had numerous conversations with Kim and Paula. Heather had also had long day time chats with Paula alone. Her questions were being answered. I however, was spending more time at work and building my team. This meant that Kim did not have the opportunity to speak to me individually. If God was going to get inside my head, he would have to use someone else, some other method.

I was using a two stage recruitment process. Stage one was to fill a conference room in a local hotel with possible candidates. I gave them a slide show and a sales pitch. At least 50% of those that came to my presentation requested an interview to come and work for me.

Peter hadn't attended any of my presentations. He just phoned me up and arranged to come into the office for an interview. He told me that he was already selling life insurance, but was looking for a new team to join. On the phone he certainly had the ability to sell himself, so we met.

As Peter had told me that he was already in the industry, I asked him the typical question that would always be asked, "How's business?" I wasn't prepared for the answer.

"Great! In fact it's never been better, since I found the Lord!"

The rest of the interview was a conversation about what Jesus had done for him. He explained that Jesus is just one step away, that he had taken that step and that his life had changed instantly. I told him about my neighbours and the reaction was as if he already knew. He continued to tell me more and more that I didn't know, that I hadn't realised.

I was so impressed with him that I gave him a job. "You can start next week" I told him, but that was the last I saw of him.

At the start of the following week, the whole team were told to clear their desks. The Government had brought in new legislation, new rules that stated our direct sales force could no longer function legally. We were all out of work.

Peter though had planted more seeds in me. Within a few weeks those seeds would grow. I would have my eyes and heart opened to God's forgiving grace, love and mercy. Later I would look for Peter. I would try to track him down, but could not find his telephone number in my diary. I would contact others from the office to ask them if they remembered him, but none of them had seen him! I now believe that this was yet another encounter with an angel. Kim and Paula had given me a lot of answers, but I was blind. God sent Peter to break down the remaining barriers and I listened.

It's interesting that the good Samaritan that I had phoned, all of those years ago, on that dark wet night when I was fifteen years old had also called himself Peter!

# Chapter Eight

## Turning point

Conversations with Kim and Paula were now becoming more frequent. Suddenly I had more time on hand. Unemployment also raised the question of "what next?"

I was offered jobs with various companies, asking me to go to them and sell insurance products, but it was time for a change.

Could I go back to building? I decided that the answer to that question would only be known if I just tried it. To try to run my own building business seemed just too risky. I would start by going on a short college course at the Gloucester Skill Centre, the 'Work Related Skills Assessment Course – WRSAC'. This was a course that looked at a whole range of skills and trades, but I was only interested in one trade, bricklaying.

I spent six weeks really teaching myself, as it seemed that I knew more than the tutor. As I did this, my confidence grew. My work was different, creative and imaginative. Before long the students on the bricklaying course were coming to look at my work. They were impressed, with some even saying that they couldn't do what I was doing. I took photographs of everything that I built and this became a portfolio that I could use to help me find work. I still strongly believe in the power of a good portfolio and have seen it open many a door for young people who are trying to find work. Whilst on this training programme I went on a crash diet and lost over two stone very quickly (wouldn't recommend this now). I was almost fasting and now understand how our spirits are stronger when we are physically weaker (Matthew 26:40-43).

Even more time was being spent talking to Kim and Paula. I remember attending a local church, as we wanted to have Ellie christened. Chris had been done, so why not? It was tradition. The 'done' thing.

The church minister explained that we may want to consider a 'dedication' rather than a christening. It sounded less formal and I suppose less religious. It sounded better, so we agreed.

We didn't want to just turn up out of the blue one Sunday, with people wondering who we were, so we started to attend the church every week. Very slowly we started to talk to people as they all seemed friendly and welcoming, at least on the surface. We had been turning up every Sunday for about four weeks, Ellie's dedication was booked for two weeks time, but at this service we left feeling very upset. It was announced that there was going to be a meeting in the following week, we couldn't believe our ears.

The meeting was to discuss the increasing number of people who were using the church, for things such as weddings, funerals, christenings and of course dedications. There was concern over the fact that these people were not committed to the church. I often think about that church and how it communicates to the world now.

I went home and had a moan at Kim. It was more than a moan, I was angry! We would have likely stayed attending this church, but this judgemental, petty attitude drove us away. We never went back after the dedication service.

Kim described what I was feeling as "Holy Anger." He explained that Jesus had become angry with the hypocrites and of what had become of 'his Father's House'. His anger had resulted in tables being turned over. Had I thought of it, I may even have turned over a few tables. That Holy Anger can still affect me today. Another seed had been sown or was it another stitch of the Golden Thread being sewn?

Having finished my short training course, I considered what the next rung of the ladder should be. "The lowest level on any building site is the labourer," I thought to myself, "so that is where I should start."

I found a job advertisement that was asking for someone to help with labouring on a huge extension project. The original cottage consisted of just one room upstairs and one room downstairs. The extension though was the size of a hotel, with woodland on one side and a lake on the other.

Arriving on site I introduced myself to the foreman, Tom. He really didn't know much about construction and was just a trusted friend of the owner. His job was to make sure that the stonemason and the carpenter had everything that they needed to do their jobs. Right now they both needed extra help with boring, strenuous, repetitive tasks and so I was there to help both.

I was keen to make an impression and so arrived on site every morning at 7.00am. This was a good hour before Andy the stonemason would arrive. By 8.00am I had loaded out the scaffolding with a selection of stone, mixed the mortar and loaded that out ready to go. Andy was old and slow, which meant that I would find myself standing around, waiting for him to catch up. It seemed to me that because of this, my boss was wasting money, so I suggested that he let me lay some stone instead of just hanging around waiting. Andy felt slightly threatened, I'm sure that he wanted to make the job last until his retirement, but my work ethic wouldn't allow that.

Now the job was progressing well and I was given my own little projects. It was whilst I worked alone on my own projects that I started to think about the conversations with Kim and Paula, about my 'Holy Anger' and other things.

On 4th May 1986 I went home and read through a small booklet that Kim had given me. It was called 'A Journey into Life' by a man called Norman Warren. Now after so long of searching... questions... answers... seeds being sown and a lot of prayer (mainly by others), things were beginning to make sense.

I went to bed contemplating what I had read. The next morning I made myself some breakfast and sat eating it whilst looking at my fish tank. I wasn't just watching them I was admiring them, admiring 'my fish'. In fact I was almost worshipping them! I did this every morning, but this morning seemed different. I was still thinking about what I had read during the previous evening. I couldn't rid my mind of it; even if I tried it was still there. Norman Warren's words had left a strong impression.

Now mixed in with these impacting thoughts, my usual thoughts also appeared. "These fish are amazing, they are so graceful and so beautiful," but as I thought this something happened.

This was the first time that I ever heard God speak to me. It wasn't a loud, booming, thundering voice, it wasn't even audible, but it was a gentle, touching presence. The words were placed directly into my mind, just like a computer download and I remember as clearly now as I did on that 5th May morning in 1986.

"Yes, they are beautiful aren't they, but don't forget that I made them." It was as simple as that. God had taken what I was thinking and given it a fresh new meaning. He was giving me a fresh understanding.

There was a real presence in the room. I realised that I wasn't alone. Jesus was just one step away. He always had been, but now I realised that that step had to be taken by me! He had been speaking to me through his messengers for long enough and the final step was mine to take.

I skipped through the 'Journey into Life' book and stopped at page six. On this page I had previously found a prayer, which I now knew that I had to say. The previous page had talked about sincerity and I couldn't have been any more sincere when I said that prayer. I invited Jesus into my life over breakfast, whilst worshipping my fish!

I didn't speak to Heather before going to work, but did so upon my return. We had just finished eating and sat down for the evening. Norman Warren had told me in his book to make sure that I tell someone that I had chosen Jesus. He also advised to do it within twenty four hours. If I didn't tell Heather now, we would later go to bed and that important time period would pass. I knew that if I left it, it would just get harder to tell someone.

"Did you see the book that Kim and Paula had given us?" I asked just touching my toes into the water.

"Yes," came the reply, she wasn't giving much away.
"Have you read it?" I asked.
"Yes, have you?" No longer was it just toes in the water, we were paddling up to our knees.
"Yes... I have..." hesitation, waiting before I ask, "Did you see the prayer near the back?"
"Y - e – s," came the slow reply.
"Did you read it?"
"Yes".
"So did I... Did you mean it?"
"Yes".
"So did I".

[The prayer referred to here can be found at the back of this book]

Heather had probably invited Jesus into her life a couple of days before me, but didn't know how to tell me. Although God made sure that we would both know what each of us had done.

At the weekend we would visit my mum and break the news to her. How would she react? Would she understand? She had been a regular church-goer, but that was all wasn't it? I had a few days to plan what to say.

Almost immediately, the people that knew me, my brother Chris and those that I worked with were asking questions. "What's happened to you? You seem different. You even sound different."

At least four people asked me this before I realised what it was. Previously I did use a lot of bad language, swearing and profanities. I had actually stopped blaspheming, using the name of "Jesus Christ" as an expletive, about a year ago. I really did want to stop using such bad language. I didn't want my children learning it. I had even introduced a swear box whilst working in the insurance office. The money was used to buy drink for the monthly office party and it never stopped anyone from swearing.

Now, three days after inviting Jesus into my life, I was working alone on a small dry stone wall project. Thinking about what people had been telling me, I now realised that I hadn't used any bad language for three days. Three days ago Jesus had come into my life and bad language left me.

The Bible says that "God gives us the desire of our heart (Psalm 37:4). My desire had been to stop swearing and I was delivered from the habit! I was different, I DID sound different, the people were right and they had noticed it. I was a new creation, the old had gone and the new had come (2 Corinthians 5:17).

The weekend was nearly here and we had planned to visit my mum and dad. We needed to tell them of our decision to follow Jesus, but what would they say? My dad had grown up in the West of Ireland, an area with strong Catholic influence. He had previously told us stories that the priest would visit the school, line up all of the children and say to them, "if yas don't behave yasilves the Divil a put horns on yas!" He had grown up in fear of God and the church.

My mum, on the other hand had always been a church-goer and encouraged us to go. She would be easier to talk to. Sitting in her kitchen I asked, "Mum do you know what a 'Born again Christian' is?" It was a way to try to draw her attention.

She answered my question with a question, perhaps that's where I get it from, "What like Cliff Richard?"
I didn't hesitate, "Yes like Cliff Richard, but also like me... like us!"

Her reaction was totally unexpected, she was overjoyed. I now realise that I act the same way when I have had a prayer answered and she had just had one answered.

She went on to tell me that she had given her life to Jesus at the Billy Graham crusade, which took place in Bristol in the 50's. She had never told me this before! To us she just religiously went to church each week, but now it seems there was a point of awakening and a conversion story! Why had she kept it quiet all of these years? Why do any of us keep it quiet? The answer to that is massive, there are so many reasons and that is probably another book in itself (maybe that will come next?).

For now though we talked about what had happened to us. This was just the start, as over the next twenty five years we would have endless conversations about our relationship with God, through Jesus.

My mum had been what I now regard as a 'Closet Christian'. She had asked Jesus into her life, but never really moved on much or so it seemed.

Mum soon started to attend the church that we were going to, Minchinhampton Christian Fellowship. This was where Kim and Paula had been disappearing to on those Sunday mornings, when we would watch from the window. We were no longer puzzled about where they went.

Mum used to tell me, "I like your church as it is so lively."
I would always reply, "lively is good, but the most important thing is that it is alive!"

This church certainly was alive. We quickly started to see what we now know to be the power of the Holy Spirit. Most weeks would include someone sharing a story about what God had been doing in their lives during the week. There was often a queue of people that were keen to share what God had done and each of them inspired others to look for the indicators of what God was doing in our lives. Every week prayers were being answered for someone, plus most weeks involved someone being prayed for and being healed or set free from their burdens.

Once a month the whole church organised a 'bring and share' lunch. It was during this time of fellowship that deeper friendships were formed. This group very rapidly became our extended family, with deeply-rooted bonds. We were accepted by everyone and were quite surprised to find many others that were the same age as us. These friendships and this group of Christians would eventually give birth to what is now known as 'The Door Youth Project'.

I soon stopped calling myself a 'Born Again Christian', as I now realised that to be a Christian, a follower of Christ, meant that you were born again.

In the Gospel of John, we can find in chapter three, the story of Jesus chatting to a man called Nicodemus. Here Jesus explains that we are first born of flesh, our human birth and then later we have the choice for a spiritual birth. It is this spiritual birth that is often referred to as being 'Born Again', but all Christians should have a spirit birth and continue to grow spiritually. Our spiritual growth comes from a continuous relationship with God and we were just starting out on what has become a remarkable relationship and an incredible journey.

# Chapter Nine

### Guided, directed and moulded

Jeremiah 18:5 says that, "God is the Potter and we are the clay." The potter works gently and carefully, moulding the clay. A push too much in the wrong direction and the whole pot will collapse in a useless mess.

I know that I have over the years been moulded by the hands of God, as he formed me to become his instrument. Although in that first year, there was such a lot to take in! I can't remember the exact sequence of events, but I do remember the stories. These stories built the foundation of my relationship with God.

### A tale of two Duncans

Within the first three months of becoming a Christian I was invited to attend a Wednesday morning prayer meeting. It started at 7.00am and it was for local Christian businessmen. Why I should have been considered for this, I wasn't quite sure? I wasn't in business I was just a labourer on a building site! Incidentally that same prayer meeting is still meeting on most Wednesdays twenty seven years on.

We would always start with coffee and sometimes toast, it was very civilized. It was called a 'prayer' meeting, but at times the Holy

Spirit would lead someone to start singing. Everyone would join in and I quickly learnt the words to many songs.

Occasionally someone would bring a scripture from The Bible and share something about what it meant to them. Then very occasionally someone might bring a prophetic word from God.

I had never heard about prophecy before. I had read about people in The Bible called 'Prophets', but didn't realise that there were still Prophets around today.

Duncan White (the 1$^{st}$ Duncan) was such a person. I really didn't know Duncan and he certainly didn't know me. Now, during the prayer time, Duncan started to speak in a way that sounded different. This was God speaking directly through him. I was partly intrigued to hear this new thing and partly amazed to think that this was God's own words for us today. He talked a lot. Far too much for me to remember every word, but the gist of what he said was, "Two of you will do great things. You will become a team, which will reach out and touch thousands of lives. You will especially touch the lives of young people in this area of Stroud!"

After the prayer meeting I was outside standing on the pavement. Duncan asked if I could spare a couple of minutes for a chat. He told me he felt that the prophecy he had brought was for me. I remember sounding a little vague and asked him to repeat it.

"Can you repeat what you said in the meeting?" It was all new to me and so he repeated the gist of what he had said earlier.

Then he said, "I am absolutely convinced that one of these people is you. You will be used in a big way by God! You will touch the lives of thousands! You will speak to thousands of young people and I am not sure, but I think the other person is Andy Morris."

I had been a Christian just a few months and this was all new to me. I listened to what he had to say. I still clearly remember the conversation that took place, but it was another four years before that prophesy started to be fulfilled. It would be four years before Andy Morris and I would open The Door Youth Project. It would then be several more years after the project was opened that this prophecy would be remembered and recognised as being fulfilled!

During these same Wednesday morning prayer meetings, we would often pray for someone called Duncan (the 2$^{nd}$ Duncan). He was known to everyone else, but I had never met him. I did know that he had gone through some difficult times and was greatly in need of prayer and so I prayed for him.

The more that I prayed for him, it seemed the more I got to know him, although I had never met him.

My time on the building site with old Andy and Tom was coming to an end. I was now beginning to have the desire to go back into my own building business. Not forgetting that God gives us the desire of our heart, I took the step.

I needed four things to start myself off. Transport was number one. I couldn't work without a vehicle and I had that. So, next was a name for my business. I wanted to be near the start of the telephone directory, so it had to start with the letter "A". As I searched in The Bible for inspiration I read, "I am the ALPHA and the Omega." I liked the word 'Alpha' and thought about what the Alpha symbol looked like. It was similar to the fish symbol that is used to say "I am a Christian." So I had a name and a logo, ALPHA BUILDING SERVICES ⵣ. Kim was a printer and a graphic designer. He produced some business cards and some headed paper for me. Now I was in business.

The third thing that I needed was a job and a very kind man called Derek Morris (yes Andy's dad) gave me my first job, to paint his house. It was a big house, so therefore a big job. Some of it would require scaffolding.

I didn't want to go on scaffolding by myself, so the fourth thing that I needed was a labourer. I prayed about this, as I had never before this employed anyone to work for my own business.

I remember that we had been invited to go to an event on the Three Counties Show Ground near Malvern. David Pawson was speaking and I was praying before going. I asked God what I should do about employing a labourer. I remember turning to my Bible after praying and read the words, "You will know him when you see him."

Upon arriving at Malvern, I was introduced to Duncan, who we had been praying for. I had already come to know him through prayer. Now as soon as we met, I felt God say, "You will know him when you see him." Duncan was to be my labourer, the fourth part of my plan for business. I had to give him a job.

I asked him if he was looking for a job, "Oh yes! Am I ever! What I wouldn't do for a job?" He sounded keen, yet desperate. "Come and see me tomorrow for an interview."

I had interviewed people for work before during my time selling insurance but never like this. I knew that I wanted to give him a job, that God wanted me to give him a job, but I also knew that he had to earn it. If he was going to work for me, he had to work his way into the job. We were friends immediately and at the end of the interview I told him that he had a job. He couldn't believe what he was hearing. It was as if I had given him a new life and that is exactly what I had done, but that is his story to tell. He was even more blown away when I disclosed to him that God had told me to give him a job, before I had interviewed him. God had answered his prayers and saved his life from the road that he was on.

Interestingly, I still often have the same feeling now, when I am interviewing someone for a job. I will often feel God say, "This is the one that I want you to employ!"

## Becoming a Capstone

We settled quickly into a new way of life and the Potter continued to mould us just like the clay. It wasn't long before we were attending mid week small group meetings. These could be in the form of a Bible study, a short course, a prayer meeting or simply a social gathering.

A few weeks before Duncan gave me his prophetic word, another word from God was given to me. That same word still resonates with me, whenever I hear it.

It was given to me at another prayer meeting, which was this time being held at Derek Morris's house. I was still working there and he brought two scriptures. One was for me and the other was for Heather. We were being welcomed into this body of believers and Derek said, "I have been praying and asked the Lord to give me a word for each of you."

I don't remember the one for Heather, but he continued by reading them both out. For me he read a passage from the book of 1Peter, but the part that really spoke to me and has stayed with me ever since is, "the stone the builder had rejected will become the Capstone" (1 Peter 2:7).

He knew nothing about my previous attempt to try to run a building business. He knew nothing about my fall and my first angel encounter and he knew nothing of the fear that I had first experienced on Eric's roof. He didn't know that I had (or so it felt) been rejected, but God knew and he understood. This was God speaking directly to me through his word and channelled via Derek's obedience, sensitivity and discernment.

That word would also be fulfilled, as over the next two years my business would grow on the wave of the building boom which was now in place. I always say that God's timing is absolutely perfect and this was the perfect time for the construction industry. By 1988 I would be employing a team of twenty seven men and managing projects over nine different sites.

God was now leading and guiding us on an amazing journey. That journey would see many signs and wonders. We would witness miracles and see prayers answered, but through all of this we would learn to trust God, grow in our relationship with him and be built up in faith.

### Tested

The Bible tells us that you "should not test the Lord your God" (Deuteronomy 6:16), although that doesn't stop him from testing us. I do believe that God tested me very early in my journey with him. At the time that it happened though, I didn't stop and say, "I think God is testing me?"

My test would teach me to "let go and let God". I did know this, but would still frequently forget what I had learnt and do things my own way. Then when something went wrong, I would say to myself, "I really must let go and let God!"

We had decorated every room in our new home next to Kim and Paula, with the exception of the spare bedroom. This room had been used as a bit of a dumping ground, but it was now time to clear the mess and start making better use of the room. It would be Chris's room. Ellie had the smaller nursery room and was asleep in her cot as we worked.

Chris was there with us and getting into all sorts of things. He was naturally inquisitive, the same as any two year old.

It was time for a break and we both went downstairs to the kitchen. We wouldn't be gone long and Chris was safe. The stair gate was in place and there was nothing to harm him. At least that is what we thought, until we returned just five minutes later.

Chris had found an old medicine cabinet and thought the contents were for eating! A two year old will naturally put anything in their mouths, with the favourites being snails and worms. The sight before us now though was more serious. The box contained potassium permanganate crystals. This is something that I had used for the treatment of 'trench foot', which I had suffered from during building work in wet conditions. All it took was a few crystals in a bowl of warm water to help dry out the feet, but the feet would be stained a dark purple colour, like wearing purple socks.

Chris had poured the contents of the container into his mouth. This intensive dose had now turned his mouth, tongue and lips completely black.

Fear passes very quickly, followed by basic survival and protection instinct. Picking him up from the floor I ran to the bathroom and started to wash out the remaining crystals, pouring water into his mouth. Another natural reaction tends to be to look for blame and now, as I washed out his mouth I started to shout out, "God why have you let this happen? God this can't be happening!" Although, it was and I lost count of how many times I said it. In my head I knew that God was almighty and all powerful, he could have stopped this. I had forgotten that we also have a responsibility as parents. We were really the ones to blame, but I failed to see it!

I ran to the car and headed for Stroud General Hospital, which was just a short drive down the hill. At the same time, Heather phoned her mum asking her to come and pick her and Ellie up. Things were happening fast and the hospital called for an ambulance to transfer Chris to the much bigger hospital of Gloucester Royal, where there was a special poisons unit.

Whilst waiting for her mum to arrive, Heather also discovered that some herbal sleeping medication had also been consumed. The situation immediately became even more serious than had previously been realised. She phoned the hospital with this new information and the nurse told her to head straight to Gloucester Royal. I heard as the nurse passed this new information to the ambulance crew and we left with blue lights flashing.

My son looked a mess and was now beginning to lose consciousness. This wasn't sleeping, he had passed out. Now at about three miles into our journey his body was limp. Until this point I had not stopped blaming God. Outwardly I tried to remain calm, whilst in my head I was still shouting, "God why are you letting this happen?"

Now my thoughts changed. I remembered that Jesus said, "Let the little children come unto me" (Matthew 19:14). This wasn't God. Then maybe it was an attack? I had read about spiritual battles between forces of good and evil. If this was evil, it didn't belong in this ambulance. It was like a revelation.

My mind suddenly became calmer. In my head I prayed, "Lord please don't let Chris die. Don't let the Devil take him, but if he does have to die, please will you take him and look after him? I place his life into your hands. Please Lord PLEASE!"

I prayed like this for the remaining seven miles of the journey, but he never moved, he remained still, his body limp.... I continued to pray.

The ambulance stopped. We stepped out into

the summer air. His eyes opened. He spoke, "Ambulance". Heather appeared with her mum. We were rushed into the poisons unit. The doctor arrived immediately. Chris spoke as he picked up the toy, "Lego." He seemed fine. God had heard and answered the prayer. I had given my son to God. He had given him back! The medics had never seen anyone swallow potassium permanganate before. His mouth, tongue and lips were still black and the doctor suggested keeping him in overnight for observation.

I said, "He's fine now, we'll take him home." I didn't give God the glory for his healing. I was a young Christian, only a month old, but I have made up for it since.

"Okay," said the doctor, "you can take him home, but he is going to look awful for at least the next two weeks. The black will take at least that long to go."

We took him home and gave him a drink of blackcurrant Ribena. Within twenty four hours the black staining had disappeared. So I look at it like this, either the doctor had been wrong, Ribena has an amazing neutralising effect on potassium permanganate or God really had healed him. I know which one I believe! Ribena would later play another part in a different story. That story would have a different ending, with a mixture of different emotions.

I later realised that a man in The Bible called Abraham had a similar story to tell, regarding his son Isaac (Genesis chapter 22).

I had grown massively through this testing time. The test didn't last long, but the memory is still strong. This would be my foundation to build upon and always to look back at. It would remind me that God is in control, but also that we have to more and more, "let go, let God!"

### God can heal

I had witnessed the healing power of God and wanted to see more.

When I was two years old, I cut my middle finger of my left hand. The nurse rushed the repair, as she was in a hurry to finish her shift. In her haste she had stitched through the tendon. As I grew older, the tendon didn't grow with me and the result is a finger that is now bent. It has become something of a trademark, but when I became a Christian I asked for prayer for it. I did this whenever there was an opportunity.

I can remember taking several photographs of my finger and thinking to myself, "when God heals my finger, I will be able to show everyone how it was and then compare it to how it looks following God's miraculous healing". Looking back now, I realise how stupid that sounds. The photograph could have been on someone else's hand. People would not believe it was mine!

Hardly a week went by when someone didn't pray for it. Sometimes the Holy Spirit would come and just gently knock me down. I found out that this is referred to as being "slain" or "resting" in the spirit and whenever it happened, I just felt cocooned in the overwhelming presence and love of God.

On one occasion Kim was praying for my finger. The Bible tells us to pray whilst laying on hands (when appropriate, touching the part that needs healing). As Kim prayed we both felt the power of the Holy Spirit. The finger became hotter and then we both felt the crack, "Did you feel that? Kim asked. He already knew the answer, as I showed him that I had movement in the end of my finger.

"I couldn't move that before!" I told him and both of us knew that God had touched my finger.

I continued to ask for prayer for my finger to be completely healed, but I stopped asking in May 1987. I had been a Christian for a whole year. I had seen my son healed and my finger had been touched by God, but never completely healed.

It's not that God couldn't heal my finger, but he

chose not to. It is a rare thing for anyone to know why God chooses not to heal and in 1987 I just accepted it. I felt that by giving me movement in part of it, God was saying, "I can do it if I want to, but I want it to stay the way that it is for a reason." I would have to wait another nine years before I would find out the reason why God chose not to heal my finger completely.

# Chapter Ten

### A new gift I give to you...

It is important to know that becoming a Christian doesn't mean that life suddenly all becomes a "bed of roses". Yes, God provides all of our needs, but we still have to work, to battle on and play our part. We would play our part by praying into situations and stepping out in faith.

Our time of living next to Kim and Paula was coming to an end. We had been there for just three and a half years and our neighbours had being praying for our salvation for most of that time!

Alpha Building Services was now becoming established with a good run of work.

The desire of our heart now was to live back up in Chalford Hill, so we put our house up for sale. Although finding a property back in this village where we had both grown up was now not that easy. Anything that we considered was quickly bought by someone else and usually for a lot more than we could afford. Would God give us our hearts' desire this time? It seemed impossible! Would the Golden Thread lead us to where we were meant to be?

We prayed about the situation. We had learnt to

pray and read The Bible following prayer. Sometimes during praying, I would feel led to a certain book in The Bible, with chapter and verse. This was God speaking to us, directing us, using his word to speak into our lives. At times when a chapter and verse didn't come, simply opening the Bible at a random point and reading what jumped off the page, would often be an answer to prayer. God had directed us in this way when I was to employ Duncan. Now praying about where we were to live he spoke to us again. The Bible fell open near the centre and Psalms 2:6 read, "Yet I have set my king upon my Holy Hill of Zion."

What did that mean? Holy Hill? Was that Chalford Hill? It wasn't that clear until the full picture was revealed. Nowadays I realise how important it is to look at the full picture. This verse in the book of Psalms was just a road sign. We would need to keep it in mind and recognise the turning, the direction to take, when the time was right!

We soon found a buyer for our house and in a strange coincidence it turned out to be Tom with the Kawazaki motor cycle. Now, thirteen years on from the crazy party that nearly ended in a lynching, Tom wanted to buy our house.

The deal was done. A price had been negotiated and solicitors were notified. The sale was all going smoothly. We still didn't have anywhere to move to and a few weeks later were starting to wonder if we would ever find anywhere? What did Psalms 2:6 mean? What were we supposed to do?

The phone rang and it was Tom, with what seemed like bad news. He had a property to sell and the sale of that had fallen through. "I'm afraid that unless I can find another buyer, I won't be able to buy your house. I don't suppose you want to buy a building plot do you?"

We had never considered a building plot. The risks were so high! We would be technically homeless again, but he had managed to grab my attention. I wanted to know more, "Where is it? How big? What's it like?"

"It's in Chalford Hill and big enough for a large four bedroom house."

Now he really had my attention, "OK what's the catch? What's it like?" It was very cheap and there was something that he wasn't coming straight out with.

"It's on an old thirty foot deep quarry which has been filled in with asbestos. It has been pile driven though." He sounded desperate.

This was the other part of the big picture. This

was also a great opportunity. My chance to become a house builder! Until now all of my contracts had been small projects. God's signpost of Psalms 2:6 had mentioned the Holy Hill in Zion. It also referred to a king. The house that we could build would be our castle (fit for a king) on top of Chalford Hill. I don't really think that Chalford is a Holy Hill, but it is a great place and the house that we would build, we would call "Zion House" and in 2014 it still has that same name.

I put down the phone after talking with Tom and discussed this option with Heather. We wasted very little time as we both knew that it was right.

The sale now proceeded quickly and we moved our entire belongings into storage at Andy Morris's Foundry.

In February 1987 we purchased a second-hand, very large mobile home and had it delivered to our new building site. With no electricity we had to rely on a generator until the main connection was made. We had no water and had to visit my mum's for a bath and to fill up water containers.

The main sewer was nearby and we quickly made a temporary connection, but we would live without water and electricity for over a month.

The man from the local council arrived on the

same day as the mobile home. "You don't have planning permission for this! You can't live here!" His tone was authoritative and he sounded rather impatient.

I thought back all of those years to a similar situation. My parents had moved into a house that had been condemned and was considered for demolition. The man from the council had arrived then and told my dad that he couldn't live there. My dad had just answered, "Okay then, you can find somewhere else for me and my family to live!" They never did and we just stayed there. So I now used the exact same reply, "Okay you find somewhere else for us to live!"

He started to calm down and became more reasonable. I explained that the mobile home was not permanent. He then told me that we would have to apply retrospectively for temporary planning consent. We did however still have to have plans drawn up and submitted to gain full and detailed planning approval. This would be for a big house!

It would actually take us eight months before we would be able to move into the unfinished house and during that time I would be visited by two very different Christian friends. Each of these would have a different approach to our situation.

We adjusted very quickly to living in a mobile home. We had done this before in Cornwall which was all good preparation for where we were now. There was of course the added complication of two small children, both under the age of four years old but they also adapted well.

With plans passed, we started the groundwork in April 1987. Every spare moment of my time was now to be consumed in building our new home. I had done this with our first house and knew what it would take. With our first house though, I wasn't a Christian. I wasn't going to church every Sunday morning. I couldn't now afford to waste time and decided that church would have to wait. Some may have said that I was 'back sliding' and 'falling away' from God, but that was not the case at all. His Golden Thread continued with me throughout the build. It may not have been visible, on the front of my 'Tapestry of Life', but it was still there. All anyone had to do was turn the tapestry over.

At the start of 1987, my friendship with Andy Morris had developed and I was now helping him with youth work in the church. He had asked for anyone to help him and I just felt that it was right to offer a hand.

Andy was a practical, helpful friend and he knew just what he had to do, as he came to see me.

My lack of attendance at the church meant that I hadn't been able to help him for a while, but he didn't judge me for not being there. "What can I do to help you? Give me a job! I'm here to help!"

I hadn't even asked him for help but he just knew that I needed it. He helped me to clean up asbestos, wheeling wheelbarrows and shovelling. He was the only one of my new found Christian 'friends' that turned up to help me. I have always had a bit of a problem with asking for help, but they all knew what I was doing. I also have the attitude that a good volunteer is worth ten 'pressed men' and Andy worked hard. We were a team! He gave me a few days of help, which in the scale of the project, didn't sound like much, but it was enough. It was practical and it said, "I understand."

My second visitor was very different. He was one of the leaders of Minchinhampton Christian Fellowship. "We're concerned that we haven't seen you on a Sunday."

I couldn't believe my ears. We were standing in the small lounge space of our temporary home, staring out at a building site. Was he totally blind? I remember the anger that I had towards him. He had a zero level of compassion! Looking back now, I can see that this man lacked the essential pastoral skills that are required. The leaders were concerned that we were 'back sliding', but if Andy Morris hadn't given us his practical help and support, we may have done exactly what they feared.

One man had judged me and I felt condemned me, whilst the other had helped. That help had tipped the balance and made me thankful. I wasn't just thankful for Andy's help, I was thankful for the provision of this house, this 'Zion House' that God had led us to. This house would become the 'jewel in the crown' for my business. It would be regarded as an excellent example of my work and it would lead others to me. They would also want houses built.

Eventually we returned to Minchinhampton Christian Fellowship, but more importantly we returned in order to return the favour to Andy. I now started to help him even more. I can remember thinking to myself, "I wish I could be as good at youth work as Andy is." He was good and I don't think I was the only one with those thoughts.

Andy was aware of how people regarded him and he would often say, "People need to stop trying to be like me!"

Eventually I also heard God, as he spoke into my heart again, "Don't try to be like Andy, be like me!" I don't know when that was, but I am glad that it happened.

We said goodbye to our mobile home and now found ourselves living in an unfinished house on a plot of land with asbestos fragments on the subsoil. Until then we had been watering the asbestos down for health and safety reasons. If it were allowed to dry out, the dust could be very dangerous to health. Our new priority therefore was to landscape the garden, burying the asbestos and making it safe. Heather was now pregnant again with our third child. Hannah would be born in February 1989 and our growing family needed somewhere that they could play safely.

We continued to learn more in mid week Bible studies and more friendships were developed. It was a continuous juggling act of what we needed to do for family, house, work and church.

One Sunday afternoon, in the spring of 1988, we had been to church and returned. We hurried through lunch in order to carry on working in the garden. The project in hand was digging out a foundation for a dry stone wall.

It was near the end of the afternoon when I decided that it was time to stop. I now sat briefly in the armchair in the unfinished lounge. Something didn't feel right, as I tried to move, pain hit me. I couldn't stand up. My back had locked up completely! I did eventually manage to lift myself from the seat, but I was still in the sitting position. Now I was bent double, with my head looking straight down into the seat that I had just managed to get out of. The pain was unbearable. In desperation, I managed to lower myself back into the chair. I then asked Heather to phone around, asking some people to come and pray for me.

Geoff Sanders, Derek Morris and Basil Sands arrived and prayed for my back to be healed. I felt that familiar, warming touch of the Holy Spirit and the pain left me. Movement returned and I was able to stand. The three 'Prayer Warriors' told me that they would need to return later in the week for further prayer and we agreed to them coming back on the following Wednesday.

In the meantime, I thought it best to seek some medical advice, just to be on the safe side. I managed to book an emergency appointment with an osteopath the next day. She told me that it was highly likely that my spine was bent, as she could see that my left leg was about an inch shorter than the right one. She did various things to try to manipulate my spine, but it was still the same when I left. She asked me to return the following week.

Derek, Basil and Geoff returned on the Wednesday as agreed. I told them about my visit to the osteopath and showed them that my leg was shorter than it should be. They first of all prayed for this leg to grow and be healed. They laid on hands as they prayed. I sat on a chair and my leg was stretched out in front of me. I remember thinking, "If my leg is going to grow I want to see it happen." So I kept my eyes open throughout.

Once again, before not very long I could feel the healing warmth of the Holy Spirit touching me. It didn't take long before my leg appeared to grow. I watched it, heard the creaking and felt it change! I quickly sat on the floor and put both legs out in front of me to check. Both legs were the same length and it felt amazing.

Derek next asked me if I had ever had any involvement with the occult. "No, not really," I replied. I had never worshipped the Devil or sacrificed animals, I was fine. He continued by asking questions about specific things that he suspected I may have 'dabbled' in. I told him about my teenage years and the séances, about the voodoo and even the horoscopes were mentioned. I told them about the detail of the séance that took place near Southampton, about the image of the old lady in the mirror and the fact that one moment it was there and the next it was gone.

Derek explained that the manifestation that I had seen was an evil spirit and that it had probably entered into me. He explained that we can breathe evil spirits in and I flashed my mind back to the moment in that room. That moment when fear struck me and I took a sharp intake of breath, then it was gone. Was I really 'possessed'?

Derek continued to explain that this spirit was now manifesting itself in my back problems, so I asked for them to pray for it to come out. They did as I asked and I was delivered! There was no dramatic thrashing around, I just breathed out as I was told to. My mouth was suddenly filled with a stale, rancid taste. I breathed it out. The foul taste lasted just a second or two.

They prayed again and I breathed in the refreshing, cleansing power of the Holy Spirit. This new power of God would manifest itself in a new form and use me in a way that I never would have imagined.

Less than a month later I was asked if I would like to be involved in an outreach mission, aimed at young people in Chalford Hill. Now that I was helping with church youth work, it made sense to say yes.

I had also recently started doing school assemblies with Rob Burr at Archway School. He would sing his songs and I attempted backing vocals.

The mission was a week long and full of fun games, music and a message. It was suggested that we use some drama with a message. Most of the material that we used for this was written by Dave Hopwood from Lee Abbey. The sketches were simple and powerful. Some of them were written in the style of 'rap', punchy, rhyming verse. Dave Hopwood explained in his books that a large group of people should all speak out the rhyme and clap their hands for a beat, whilst the story was told in the form of mime and actions. We didn't have a large group of people but we tried it anyway, with just two people rapping and clapping. I sat and watched, never really wanting to put myself forward. It didn't sound very good!

Dave Rose had been asked to have a go at it with someone else. I'd seen Dave a few times at church, he was quite new as well and he told me that he had a musical interest, having been in a few bands. He was good, but the other person was struggling.

When I had become a Christian, soon afterwards I felt that God led me to get rid of my record collection. I had worshipped it for too long and it had become my false god. I felt that God was saying, "Get rid of that 'false god' and I will give you something much better." I had also been a drummer in a few bands and could sing reasonably well.    Maybe performance was another one of my heart's desires?

Now, everyone in the room realised that this rap duo wasn't working.  They all turned to me and asked, "Do you want to try?"

"I don't know if I will be any good," I tried to defend myself before I knew.  Did I have the confidence to do this?

The person that had been partnering with Dave commented, "You can't be any worse than me, give it a go."  It was the encouragement that I needed.

I asked if we could do alternating lines.  I would take the first line and Dave the next.  Instead of clapping we used 'human beat-box' (making drum beats with your mouth).   Dave was surprised to find someone else that could beat-box.  The piece was called 'The Prodigal Rap' and three people would mime the actions.   To my surprise and probably everyone else's, it sounded good, it had potential.

A couple of weeks later Dave arrived at rehearsals with a backing track and suddenly the whole piece took on a completely different nature.  It was now more dynamic, professional and polished.  In fact it was so good that Dave Hopwood found out about it and asked for a copy of the backing track. We gave him more than that, as by then we had also recorded it with a vocal track and we shortened the title to 'Prod Rap.'

### *Prod Rap*

*Now a few years back there was a wise old man,*
*Lived on a Ranch had a clapped out van.*
*Had two strong sons and life was swell,*
*A hen, three gerbils and a wife as well.*

*But one fine day working in the rough,*
*The youngest boy said, "I've had enough!"*
*Threw down his spade on his brother's toe*
*And headed for his father just to let him know.*

*He packed his bags and he stood at the door,*
*Said, "digging aint what my right arm's for!"*
*"Don't try to stop me, cuz I'm gonna go,*
*Gonna get me some fun, if you give me some dough!"*

*It was a mean old day for the poor old man,*
*Cuz he loved his son and couldn't understand.*
*Why he wanted to leave his family and home,*
*But he gave him all his money and he watched him go.*

*Well, I'd be lying if I didn't tell you,*
*He had a lot of fun – for a week or two.*
*Laughing, dancing, drinking homebrew.*
*The cars were fast and the girls were too.*

*Till one fine day he woke up in a daze,*

127

*Smelling worse than the neighbourhood strays.*
*His body was aching and his brain was bad,*
*His friends had run off with everything he had.*

*Nobody cared now that he was broke,*
*His life had become a mighty bad joke.*
*Lost all he had and when he fell asleep,*
*Someone stole the fillings from his two bad teeth.*

*Well he felt pretty silly and he wandered around,*
*Till he got so thin his pants fell down.*
*So he took a job dishing out pig swill,*
*And it smelt so bad that it made him ill.*

*Then suddenly he realised,*
*What a fool he'd been and he opened his eyes.*
*He saw the waste, his life had become,*
*Lost everything for a week of fun.*

*"I'll go on home", he said that day,*
*I'll scrub the floor for a servant's pay.*
*"What a fool to reject my dad!*
*Couldn't see just what I had."*

*Well he walked on home in the mid-day sun,*
*It was the hardest thing he had ever done.*
*He was a broken man now, nothing to lose,*
*The holes in his life like the holes in his shoes.*

*He threw himself at the feet of his dad.*
*Said "Dad I've wasted everything I had.*
*I know I've done wrong and you should send me away,*

128

*But if I work for you will you let me stay?"*

*"Son I love you," the father replied,*
*I thought you were lost, I figured you'd died.*
*It broke my heart, when you went away,*
*And I've been waiting for you to come home today.*
*I don't care where you've been or what you've done,*
*I just want you back, cuz you're my son."*

Performing felt good. It felt very good! I was now a rapper, but where would it lead?

Dave would soon come to work for me. He was the kind of person that changed his job every year. I was expanding my business and needed another labourer. Duncan had now left and moved on into nursing (he was better suited to that). Working with Dave would help us to develop a musical partnership with extremely strong chemistry.

The summer of '88 was coming to an end and plans were already being made towards Christmas. The Oasis Trust had launched a campaign called 'Christmas Unwrapped'. We had been looking at it briefly, considering whether the group of young people that we were now working with would want to get involved. It was enough to plant a seed of thought.

I found myself in another big prayer meeting at Derek Morris's house. As we prayed, the words

129

of a song kept coming into my head...

*It's Christmas, Christmas,*
*Christmas unwrapped, Christmas unwrapped.*
*It's Christmas, Christmas,*
*Christmas unwrapped for you.*

*Whose party is it anyway?*
*I hear you say on Christmas.*
*I don't really care, just have a good time,*
*with turkey, tinsel and plenty of wine.*

The words continued over and over in my head and I had a feeling that I had heard this song before. It had a certain familiarity to it. When I left to go home, it was still going around in my head. I was trying to think where I may have heard it, but could not come up with an answer. I found it quite frustrating.

The next morning Dave arrived at my house before we headed off to work on a site together. I asked him if he recognised this song. The words were still very clear in my head and now even stronger. I told him that this song had been in my head since the prayer meeting of the previous evening, but couldn't think where I may have heard it?

"I reckon you heard it last night, when God gave it to you," Dave said with a smile on his face. I wasn't sure what he was saying, so asked him to clarify.

"God has given you a song, it's yours, I've never heard it until now, so I reckon you ought to get and finish writing it!"   I had not recognised God's voice speaking these words into me.  This was the first time I had ever experienced this, but it wouldn't be the last.

We went to work, but as we worked I had to keep stopping.  Every so often more words would come into my head.  Verse after verse, until by mid afternoon, when we stopped for a cup of tea, it was almost finished.  One line was missing and together we wrote that.  Dave wrote the backing track and together we had finished our first song.  Christmas Unwrapped would be remixed in different styles over the next twenty six years and it would be heard by over 25,000 people.

### *Christmas unwrapped*
***Chorus****: It's Christmas, Christmas,*
*Christmas unwrapped, Christmas unwrapped.*
*It's Christmas, Christmas,*
*Christmas unwrapped for you.*

*Whose party is it anyway?*
*I hear you say on Christmas.*
*I don't really care, just have a good time,*
*with turkey, tinsel and plenty of wine.*
*It's Christmas, Christmas,*
*Christmas unwrapped for you.*

*There'll be gifts on the tree and mistletoe,*
*Toys, nuts, cards, cake, booze, holly and snow.*
*We'll party all night, we'll party all day,*
*Whose party is it anyway?*

*Chorus*

*We'll rock the house this time of year,*
*We celebrate with party cheer.*
*We'll party all night, we'll party all day,*
*Whose party is it anyway?*
*It's Christmas, Christmas,*
*Christmas unwrapped for you.*
*Carol singers sing and sleigh bells ring,*
*There's plum pudding and everything.*
*There's party fun, for everyone.*
*What's that, I hear you say?*
*Whose party is it anyway?*
*Chorus*

*Well I could tell you some more*
*about these joyous things,*
*But this you already know!*
*So I'll tell you 'bout the truth and*
*I'll tell 'bout the way,*
*That you must surely go.*
*So stop as I unveil to you what it's really all about,*
*'bout giving an loving an peace on earth an that's*
*without a doubt.*
*It's Christmas, Christmas,*
*Christmas unwrapped for you.*
*Just take a look at the Holy Book and*

*you will find the way,*
*God sent his son into the world,*
*upon that Christmas day.*
*"Emmanuel" they called him, God with us!*
*He sent his son into the world to save us.*
*It's Christmas, Christmas,*
*Christmas unwrapped! X3*
*For you and you and you and you and you...*

To recognise God's voice takes practice and unless we practise listening, we never will. I was now keen to hear God speak to me more. I was excited about the opportunity to have another song to perform. The 'Prod Rap' was good, it had been fun and whet my appetite for rap music, but it wasn't my lyrics.

The excitement was building and I was praying to God, asking him where it would lead? He didn't answer or at least I didn't hear, that is until I was trying to sleep. I realise now that God has a habit of doing things in his timing, on his terms.

Now, as I lay in my bed, new lyrics started to pour into my head. I knew instantly that it was new lyrics, words from God, a new song, but I was tired. As my eyes closed and sleep started to fall upon me, the lyrics would drift away. I remember thinking, "I will write this song in the morning", but God had other plans. I now know that when God speaks through you, you don't mess around, just get on with it. After all, God's timing is perfect!

I lost count of how many times I had woken up and as I did the lyrics would flood back into my head, it was at least six times, maybe more. I had no choice than to get out of bed and write. Making my way downstairs I sat at my desk and the pen flowed. Out came the words and I didn't stop until the song was finished. This time it was written in one fast-flowing, non-stop session unlike Christmas Unwrapped which had taken me all day a bit here and a bit there. I wanted to listen! It was as if I was totally tuned in and I just wrote.

After I had stopped writing I didn't bother to read what I had written. I was tired, "Can I go to bed now please God?" No more words came. I knew it was the end, it was finished. Sleep!

The next morning I read what I had scribbled out in my sleepy state of mind. I was amazed by what I had written. Yes it was a new song, but it was more! God had given me a name that he wanted me to use as a rapper. The lyrics also reminded me that although God wanted to use me, he was in charge, he was the 'Master' and I was to be his MC (Master of Ceremonies or Mic Controller). The song that he had given me this time was 'The Master's MC'.

### Master's MC

*Ya'll listen right now cuz they've given to me,*
*The microphone and a chance to be free.*
*If you listen to the words, the things I have to say,*
*The smart ones among you are sure to find the way,*

*Chorus:*
*I'm the Master you see, of the ceremony*
*Now they've given me the MIC*
*I'm the Master you see, the Master's MC*
*Check it out!*

*Now the Master of the Master's MC*
*Is the Master himself, the Master JC*
*We all have a Master of some kind or another*
*But the Master I got, I can call my brother*

*Chorus*

*Some people worship the colour TV*
*Listen to their music on the latest CD*
*There's football, cricket, all kinds of sports*
*Going to the pub drinking beer and shorts*
*Maybe your master's some kinda new drug*
*Or cigarettes, you've been hit by the bug.*
*You could have the master of crime,*
*Do time you slime and other words that rhyme*

*Chorus*

*So let me tell you bout the Master JC*
*He cares for you and he cares for me.*

*He's with you at work, he's with you at play,*
*He'll tell you the truth, he'll show you the way.*
*So if you're sitting by the TV,*
*or you're sitting in the pub,*
*Remember Master JC,*
*he's the one that they call love.*
*If you're feeling kinda lonesome and*
*you want someone to care*
*Reach out to the Master, cause he is always there!*
*And that's a fact!*
*Chorus*

# Chapter Eleven

### Rise and fall

Throughout 1988 and the start of 1989, Alpha Building Services grew. The building industry was experiencing a huge boom across the country. If work came in, I just increased the workforce to cope with the demand. At the peak of the boom, I was building five different executive style houses and had smaller contracts on four other sites. In total I was running nine different sites and employing twenty seven men, all working for me and all depending on me to pay their wages every week. My job now involved driving around the sites, checking on work standards, ordering materials and keeping the money coming in. The stone the builders had rejected had become the 'Capstone' – the word that Derek had given had been fulfilled.

It was the keeping the money coming in that was becoming a problem. It doesn't take much to cause an interruption in cash flow and now I was experiencing a regular interruption. My biggest customer, a property developer started to negotiate over his invoice every month. This developer was struggling because the wave of the building boom was rapidly coming to an end. The whole building industry was heading in the opposite direction. It was about to crash.

Work started to dry up. All over the country building sites were being closed down, with half-built houses everywhere. Builders and developers were going out of business. People couldn't pay their mortgages due to high interest rates. Thousands of people had their homes repossessed by the mortgage company. I made a tough decision. Ten of my loyal workforce had to go. I was now down to seventeen men. Shortly after this move, I parted company with the developer that was bleeding me dry. I have since then learnt a lot more about business, but you could say that I learnt the hard way. How much more could I handle? How much further would it fall?

I held out as long as I could, before laying-off the next ten members of my team. This time it was harder. The first ten to go were the weaker ones; they didn't work so hard and didn't have families or mortgages. This second group of men would struggle! Some may not find another job and some may even lose their homes. I waited as long as I could, which I now know (with hindsight) was too long. I was paying wages, but didn't have the work for this fantastic gang of workers, I had no choice. This was another week, in which I added ten more to the rapidly rising number of unemployed. I should have done it weeks ago, as the delay had cost me hugely!

The stress and worry was growing. How much more could I handle?

Every time that I cut down my workforce, it just wasn't enough. The building industry was crashing faster and faster. Five more of my team had to go, which would leave just myself and Dave again – right back where I had started, only now I had two vehicles on lease hire. I couldn't afford to keep the pickup truck that also had to go. It was replaced by an old beaten up truck, what a come down! I asked myself, "Is this it? Is this the bottom? Can I fall any further?" It wasn't long though before we realised that the lease hire car also had to go. It seemed as if everything was slowly slipping away, but now we experienced something new. Rob Burr knew of our escalating financial problems and that we now had transport problems, "I've got an old car that you can have and it should keep you going for a while." This was the first car that we had ever had given to us, but it wouldn't be the last.

* * * *

There is a saying, "It was the straw that broke the camel's back!" We say it when problems and issues have piled up over a period of time and then it only takes one small thing, for everything to come crashing down. My piece of straw was a retaining wall that was moving. Dave and I had built it and we had to return on numerous occasions to carry out remedial works in order to stabilise it. The pressure was increasing as the problem was becoming unbearable. I tried not to show it, but all this did was increase the pressure even more.

I was starting to think, "I can't take any more of this!" It had been fifteen years since I had considered going to the train track and ending it forever. Now I was considering it again. The trains ran past the problem job. From the viaduct I could look down at my wall. I would put an end to this pain once and for all.

That is what I was feeling and that is what I was planning, but obviously didn't go through with it or I wouldn't be writing this now! Instead I talked to people. God pulled me back from the brink again. How could I even have considered what I was thinking? I had three young children and had been a Christian for three years, but pressure had built. It needed to be released. Talking may not sound like much, but it is an amazing way to release the pressure. Talking can be tough, but twice it had now saved my life.

I never did get another call about the retaining wall. Perhaps we had solved the problem? It is still there and I am still here. It's easy to look back and say, "No problem is ever bad enough to turn to suicide." It is a completely different matter though, when your mind is overwhelmed and can see no other way out. Anyone that has ever been there will relate to what I am saying. To those that have never been there, I sincerely hope that you never will, but if you do happen to find yourself there, go talk to someone, anyone, just talk!

Psalm 23 tells us that we can walk through the valley of the shadow of death. I had walked in that valley. It also says, "I shall not want and he refreshes my soul".

### A new plan I give you

A new feeling was building inside of me, one of a desire to give back. With less building work to do, I could now spend more time doing youth work. I was now working with young people at church on a Sunday morning and a mid week meeting. We also met regularly for Sunday afternoon walks, games and tea, but I still wanted to do more. Boys Brigade had played an influential part of my teenage years. John and Brenda Evans had been my mentors and supported me when I was younger; now looking back I was beginning to see just how much they had helped me. So I decided that it was time that I went back to help out as a leader. It had been fifteen years since I had left and it did feel good to return.

There was a growing problem of young people hanging out on the streets getting bored; Boys Brigade gave a positive focus and a hope. I would run the band sessions, teaching drums and bugles. I would also help with other activities such as first aid or planning a route for the Duke of Edinburgh Award expedition. The evening would always have a physical part such as football, circuit training or even aerobics, all of which I would organise. It was fun, but the best part was watching young people achieve something.

John and Brenda Evans were my mentors, but little did I know that I would go on into full-time Christian work. For now, I was working with them as a volunteer and mentoring young people. Interestingly at least two of those young people that I mentored at Boys Brigade have grown up to become full-time Christian workers. Anton would become a youth worker and Andrew would become a Church Minister. I believe that we all influence those that we meet, whether we spend a long time or just a brief period with them, we can plant a seed in their lives. I only stayed at Boys Brigade for two years before God called me into the next project.

The church youth group were keen to play an active role in making a difference and the Oasis Trust now had another project that they were promoting. Crackerteria encouraged groups of people to set up a temporary restaurant or cafe in order to raise funds for the developing world. It was run during December for the run up to

Christmas, hence the title 'Crackerteria'. The project had the theme of 'pay more eat less'. Our group made simple soups and curries and opened for the two weekends prior to Christmas. Alongside this, Andy and I would go out onto the streets with mince pies and entice people in.

It was so successful that we ran it for two years (1989 & 1990) and would probably still be running it now, if we hadn't been led to do something even more challenging. I do know that other projects are still running all these years later.

It was during our second year that our experience out on the street took on a whole new dimension. It was the night of the local youth club Christmas disco and there were some two hundred young people on the streets of Minchinhampton. Some had been consuming large amounts of alcohol, which was resulting in a number of aggressive situations developing. Fights were about to break out. Armed with a tin of mince pies each, Andy and I would walk into a heated situation as a punch was about to be thrown. Stepping between the potential fighters we simply said, "Happy Christmas, have a mince pie!" This was such a random thing to do, it instantly defused the aggression, often with the pair of aggressors repeating what we had just said, "Happy Christmas," they would say and sometimes even hug each other.

I have, since this experience, used this method of diversion on the streets on many occasions. Many years on from the 'Crackerteria' project I would be involved in detached youth work and would adopt this same tactic. Mince pies would become lollipops and these would be used to divert young people from fighting, but also just as a great thing to share. I found that if I was sucking on a lolly and I gave one to a young person, suddenly we would have something in common. From that point we could chat and be surprised that we had much in common. I have used various things over the years, in order to try to obtain that common link, but lollipops are my favourite as they last longer and are very cheap. I now often ponder over the number of fights and therefore arrests that have been prevented simply by sharing a lolly.

Whilst we were spending our time working with this great group of young people, working on 'Crackerteria' projects and other fun things throughout the year, the Stroud Town Council carried out a survey. This survey asked young people who were hanging around on the streets of Stroud, particularly on a Friday and Saturday evening, what they would like provided for them. Over two hundred young people then used the street as a social gathering place so it wasn't surprising that they asked for somewhere safe and friendly where they could gather. Their first choice was a Cinema for the town, which incidentally it now has. Their second choice was a Coffee Bar type of project, somewhere they could meet and not be hassled to buy anything or be moved on.

Those who were working with young people in the area were all very excited. At last young people were being asked what they wanted. Their opinions were being considered and someone would now provide what they were requesting! It was the talk of the town, but that was as far as it went 'talk' and no one did anything! Why ask? Why expose the need? Why bother if you can't follow through?

Andy Morris and I were two of those youth workers who were talking about what was going to be provided for young people. "Someone is going to provide a coffee bar for the youth of Stroud", but no one ever did!

### Following the vision

I have now learnt to identify and act upon a God-given vision sooner than I did in 1989. I had only been a Christian for three years. Andy had only been a Christian for a few months more than me and we were both still spiritual babies. Even when God had given us both the same picture, we still didn't react!

It was the summer of 1989. The findings of the

Town Council survey had been published in the local newspaper. Now whenever either Andy or I drove past a particular building, we would see it as the place where the coffee bar would be set up. The young people of the town had asked for it, so it was surely going to happen.

Twenty six Gloucester Street had recently become vacant and the two of us found it impossible to drive past without seeing the building overflowing with young people. This was not just an idea, more than just imagination running wild, this was a physical picture of what this place was going to become. Not what it could be, but what it would be! The two of us talked about this shared 'vision' that God had given us both. We agreed that this was going to be the place that someone would set up a coffee bar for young people. It would be fifteen months before we realised that God was speaking to us and eighteen months before we actually did anything.

Looking at our situation now I think that we were a little like Jonah. God spoke to Jonah and told him to go to Ninevah, but he went in exactly the opposite direction. In a similar way we did nothing about it, we just talked!

We were now doing various school assemblies that involved singing and acting. We did one song called, "When God speaks you've gotta do it!" I often now think of that song and I tend to take steps of faith more readily nowadays.

### *When God speaks you've gotta do it*
*There's a word in The Bible some people do ignore,*
*And others turn away.*
*This word is very simple it's easy to understand,*
*So let me tell you what this word does say.*
*Chorus:*
*You gotta do it, do it, do it not just hear it.*
*You gotta do it, do it from your heart.*
*When God speaks you gotta do it, do it,*
*do it not just hear it,*
*do it, do it from your heart.*

*A story in The Bible, a man walking down the road,*
*Some robbers came and punched him on the nose.*
*They took all of his money, let's clear off they said,*
*And left him there half dead.*

*Then a priest came and saw him,*
*walked passed ignored him.*
*Along came a Levite, who ran off in sheer fright.*
*Then a man from Samaria said,*
*"here mate I'll take care of ya."*
*And the man said,*
*"I don't understand why you're doing this for me.*
*So the man said, "well when God speaks..."*

*Chorus*

*A man in The Bible, Noah was his name,*

*God spoke to him one day.*
*Said, "I'm gonna send down lots of water,*
*I think I'll call it rain,*
*So build a big boat Noah and*
*you'll be saved that way."*

*So Noah wasn't lazy,*
*but his friends thought he was crazy.*
*They mock at him and laughed at him and said,*
*"You must be a nutter Noah,*
*to build a boat this way!"*
*And Noah said, "Well when God speaks...."*

*Chorus*

It was now 1990 and two friends, Ian Sadler and Rob Burr decided to re-launch the Stroud Youth for Christ organisation. This was giving Andy and me the motivational spiritual kick that that we both needed. I was thirty years old, the same age that Jesus was when he started his ministry. What better age to start something new?

I don't remember much about the Stroud Youth for Christ re-launch. Someone from British Youth for Christ was speaking, talking about the 'Remnant'. I can't remember the exact Bible verses, but the gist of what he was saying is that we would rise up out of the remnant of what was left previously. Stroud Youth for Christ had not been active for a number of years, but there were a handful of people that would soon actively

148

make that change.   The small church building was packed!

At the end of the meeting people were asked to let their names be known if they would want to do something to support the youth of Stroud. Andy and me put our names down and agreed to attend a meeting that was planned for later that week.   Interestingly, some of those who had been talking about doing something for a couple of years had failed to turn up.   I do feel that it is important that we do talk the talk and walk the walk, but sadly some will talk about doing then never actually put words into action.   Those that were present were the ones that would make something happen.   We were the remnant with enough energy and enthusiasm to rise up.

On the evening of the follow-up meeting, we started in prayer and then Andy and I shared our vision for a coffee bar.   Everyone present was excited about what they were hearing.   Nobody else had anything else to offer as a means of restarting Stroud Youth for Christ.   After talking things through for probably about an hour, we decided to pray some more.   We were now seeking the finer detail for the next steps.   After praying, Andy spoke first and said, "I think we should call it 'The Door'".

Tracy Baker (later married and became Spiers) was a BBC Radio Gloucestershire reporter and a very good person to be present. She suggested, "How about 'The Open Door'"? Other suggestions were now being thrown in for consideration such as 'Doorway'.

Just for a laugh I said, "How about 'A Jar'"? Everyone then looked at me strangely so I said, "When is a door not a door? Answer, when it's 'A Jar'". My level of humour still hasn't changed much.

Andy spoke again, "No I feel that God wants just 'The Door', as in Jesus said, 'I am The Door'. 'The Door', nothing else"! When he had finished speaking everyone agreed, we will set up a coffee bar called 'The Door'.

We were also planning our second Crackerteria, so nothing much happened until the New Year. We had no Business Plan, no money and not a lot of experience, but we had a huge heart and a pile of faith.

I talked briefly with Andy on the phone and agreed. "We've waited long enough, now it's time for action! It's time to make a phone call to the owner of twenty six Gloucester Street, the building of our vision".

Andy made the call. We had cheekily decided on a very low offer of rent. We told the owner that we wanted it for a year and that we didn't want to pay anything for six months. We were very surprised when he agreed to all of what we had asked for. He was keen to see the building used, as it had been empty for at least two years. He also wanted to see something done to support young people.

Andy called me back. As the phone rang I remember thinking that it must be bad news, it was too quick. We were both blown away at how easily it had gone, but it could have been down to the amount of prayer that had gone on before the phone call.

Two months went by as legal issues were taken care of and we were given the keys at the start of March 1991.

The building was previously used as a pine furniture shop. The previous tenant had left in such a hurry that they just made a huge hole in the floor, through which they passed everything from the basement! The building was a mess, but we had the skills to do what was required.

Andy had previously renovated an old house and was a skilled pattern maker, who owned his own foundry. My knowledge of buildings saved us having to employ a builder. We organised regular work parties, never paying for any labour and wherever we could, we would even scrounge materials.

Andy built the coffee bar and kitchen area, whilst Rob Burr made a window seat. We even roped my dad in to help with his plastering skills and he set to repairing a ceiling. An army of volunteers helped with decorating and together this great team transformed the ground floor and basement.

My work was now very sporadic and I would have about three days paid work each week. This meant that I could give the rest of my time to work on the refurbishment works that were required to keep The Door project on track. I would take Dave along with me and pay him, but I was not earning anything. Floors needed laying, walls needed building and it seemed that every task was bigger than we had first realised.

The youth group from church arrived every Wednesday evening, as they worked their way through a list of jobs. Before long we were joined by other adult groups, all of them were keen to see this project come into being.

We were now attracting helpers from many local churches and word was spreading. We were seeing volunteers from two Christian Fellowships, the Baptist Church and the Anglican Church; people from a variety of backgrounds all with one common aim, to help young people!

The refurbishment work took us about six months to complete and about a month before we opened, we invited people from the local churches to come and visit. Our thought was that if every Christian in the area could give just £1 each month, we would be able to run this thing. We were about to start paying our rent and we had no money, just a lot of faith.

The Bible says, "God shall supply all of our needs (Philippians 4:19)." People will often confuse their 'wants' with 'needs' and then wonder why they don't receive what they want. We had spent eighteen months running away from this project, so it would seem that we certainly didn't want it. Now though, we had been brought to the place of meeting the needs of young people and God was going to supply all of our needs!

In that first meeting we were pleased to see about twenty people turn up. Most of these would become the volunteer workforce. The building work was coming to an end and the real work was about to start.

We knew of no other project like this in existence and therefore couldn't go and learn from anyone else. We therefore made it up as we went along. Nowadays it's the complete opposite, as there are projects like ours all over the country. Many of those have visited us before setting up and I have always given them the same five key points for advice:

*Always involve young people in the planning, preparation and refurbishment stage.*

*Recruit an army of willing volunteers, some of whom must have the essential skills required to do the work.*

*Find at least one local business to support you. DM Foundries continued with their support for years, as they supplied our toiletries and stationery.*

*Unless you have your own charity number, set up under the banner of an existing charity. British Youth for Christ worked for us.*

*Prayer – I usually only say this one if it is a Christian group that is visiting us, although prayer is the most essential ingredient. Without it we would never have opened "The Door"!*

# Chapter twelve

### First contact

We eventually opened on the last weekend of August in 1991. We had installed a pool table, pinball table and jukebox. It was all second hand, but it was enough to attract every kind of young person that would normally be hanging around the streets. Initially to attract young people we went out to them. We gave out vouchers for free coffee and cake. We had publicity through the local press and had mentioned it during Archway School assemblies, which I was now doing with Dave and Andy.

We didn't have to wait very long until our vision of the building overflowing with young people was fulfilled. Word spread quickly. This was something new. No membership or identification was required. It was un-territorialised; no-one had made a claim on it. It was there for all young people.

The place could hold about sixty people and that would be very full but in our second weekend we saw 120 to 150 people on the Friday and Saturday. This was the vision, it was overflowing. If we had known in advance what we were getting into, we never would have stepped out on this journey. This was the start of what has now been a twenty-three year journey.

Reality started to hit us almost immediately. The demand was more than we had ever imagined. Now we began to realise just how much time this was going to take out of our lives. Andy and I both volunteered to work for three Saturdays out of four. This was a huge commitment. It took our family time. It took over our lives. Even when we weren't actually working at the project, we were still thinking about it and the young people that we were now forming relationships with. We were meeting young people with problems and struggled to switch off, unable to think about anything else. The work was all absorbing and none of us were getting paid. The project would be entirely dependent on volunteers for nearly five years.

The Stroud Town Council survey had highlighted a need for somewhere warm and dry where young people could hang out. Now we were quickly realising that some of the young people that we were meeting had much deeper needs. Some had so many problems that life had dumped on them that they just needed to unload.

None of us then had any formal training. We just wanted to help these young people, to show them that someone cared about them and most of all, to demonstrate love in action. I would think back to my own childhood, my aggression, the pain, the harm that I did to myself, the problems with the police and my many personal struggles. Being a teenager was not easy, I knew that and I empathised with them. If they wanted to talk, I was willing to listen!

It was the second weekend of opening, when a young girl asked if she could speak to a female member of staff. We hadn't met her before, no relationship had been built, but she found herself in a desperate situation and recognised that we might be able to help. She suspected that she might be pregnant. She was fifteen years old and full of fear and worry. Thinking on our feet, someone ran to the local pharmacy and we offered her a free pregnancy test. The test was negative and her world was returned to normal. Lessons had been learnt on both sides. She learnt that she would take greater care in future. We realised that we needed to provide more to meet this kind of need. Later we developed links with the local Pregnancy Crisis Centre and they would carry out any tests that were required, plus provide the right kind of support and guidance.
Over the years we have always tried to identify and meet the needs of young people that we have met. At times this has been frustrating, as needs are identified, but we are unable to do anything to help. Often the reason that we can't help is due to lack of funding!

A month after opening we held our very first business meeting. This was the first time that I had the privilege to meet Di Rowe. She had moved into the area twelve months previously and she felt that God had told her not to get involved in anything in the area until now. She explained that she was a qualified, fully accredited Christian counsellor, with experience of working with young people and families. The timing was perfect but then God's timing always is! We agreed that Di should start and head up a completely free and confidential counselling service in the flat above the coffee bar. It was a drab space but with a lick of paint, a second hand three piece suite and an old carpet that didn't quite fit, it would soon become more comfortable. This new service would eventually grow to four counsellors, receiving referrals from social workers, doctors and schools, as well as general enquires through the coffee bar. Another service that was completely free and confidential. We never would have reached the point that we are at today if it were not for so many volunteers. We still rely so much on volunteer help but at the start, it was all that we had.

Our times of opening would change over the first five years, depending on the volunteers available. Initially the coffee bar only opened on a Wednesday and Friday after school, Saturday in the day time and Friday and Saturday evenings. Each shift was manned by a different team and each team did their best to interact in a variety of different ways with the young people, but it lacked continuity!

This was a long way from Boys Brigade. It was informal, no uniform, never knowing what to expect, no membership, no restrictions on gender. We all quickly learnt the skill of improvisation. I still consider this to be one of the key skills for any youth worker.

This type of youth work soon became referred to as "off-street work". The skills that were needed were similar to working with young people on the street but now there was more of them, all gathered in one place. Some of those that we now started to see were some of those we had met nearly two years ago on the streets of Minchinhampton. They recognised both Andy and me, referring to the night that we had given them all mince pies. They remembered the aggression and told us that some big fights were planned for that night, but because of our improvisation with mince pies, peace prevailed. Now I often wonder "what is the worst thing that we have prevented?" Only God can answer that one. The presence of that Golden Thread was more powerful than we could imagine.

It was also during that first month of opening the coffee bar that we decided we needed to sell our house. Zion House, the place that God had led us to. Our debts were far too big to ever be able to pay off without doing this. We needed to sell, but it wouldn't be easy. It wouldn't be quick. We would have to learn patience and would learn to trust God in many new ways. Twenty one months would pass before a buyer would be found!

With the house on the market and after just two months of opening The Door, I felt that God wanted me to venture into full-time work for him. My building work was drying up and doors were opening that were leading me into youth work as a full-time career. One particular door that opened was an advert in the local newspaper which asked people that had been unemployed for more than six months to consider training in a youth and community course. I wasn't unemployed and should not have been allowed to qualify, but I was allowed to join. Another door opened and led me to work in a County Council youth club working with seven to twelve year olds after school, a kind of "latch key kids' club". Another opportunity was offered to me, to work in a local day centre for people with mental health issues. I worked just with young people who were struggling to cope with life. It was a huge learning curve.

It was now January 1992 and I stood up in front of the church, telling them all that I believed "God is calling me". They understood and they supported me. I was living by faith. No fixed wage. I had signed on to state benefits in order to have some form of income, but it wasn't enough. Our bank overdraft was a huge £20,000 debt, due to people that hadn't paid me and due to delaying cutting down my building workforce. Working and living by faith, I knew that God would provide all of our needs and it really was amazing what he provided. Yes, he used people, obedient servants, but he knew exactly what we needed and when we needed it.

Every so often roughly every fortnight, someone would hand me an envelope. The delivery person would tell me that someone had asked them to pass this on. It may have been another person that had given them the envelope and wished to remain anonymous, but it could have also been that God had spoken directly to them, asking them to give it to us as a blessing. We truly were blessed in what we considered to be an abundance as each envelope contained large sums of money, often hundreds of pounds.

We were only just getting by, managing to survive, money was always tight. If any unexpected expenditure happened we would never survive. The unexpected inevitably always happens and our unexpected need was related to the car again. It was a generous offer that Rob had given us his car, but it was in need of serious maintenance, full of rust but at least it worked. However, the legal requirement of the annual MOT was due. The trip to the local garage revealed the unsurprising news, the vehicle was no longer road-worthy and the cost of repairs would be excessive. We gave the car back to Rob and he presumably scrapped it.

We had managed to somehow scrape together £300 which we planned to spend on a cheap 'Banger' of a car. We knew that we wouldn't see much for our money, but it was all that we could possibly afford. We decided to take a trip in to town and drew the money out of the bank in readiness to make a quick purchase. I safely placed the money in my wallet just as Derek Morris walked up the street. He asked what we were doing and we told him of our situation. "I've got a friend that runs a garage. Don't buy anything until I have spoken to him."

We returned home and later that day Derek phoned, "he has something that is suitable, just pay him the £300 and the car is yours."

As we drove to the garage we really didn't know what to expect. On arrival we were shown an Austin Maestro with a price tag of £950. We couldn't believe what we were being offered; for the second time in our lives we were being blessed with the gift of a car. We continued to live by faith and we were continuously blessed as God provided our needs, which were being channelled through the obedience and generosity of his people.

This car was a real blessing, however it wasn't long before we needed to replace the exhaust pipe which had almost broken in half and sounded like a tractor. In a short space of time we would be unable to drive it. We told nobody of this specific need, we had already been given so much, but I did enquire how much a new exhaust pipe would cost. I was told that it would be £76.32 and realised that this was money that we didn't have! Most of what we were being given as gifts was being used to pay off debts and the mortgage, with any left being used for basic foods.

I decided to just pray and ask God to help. I told him that without the car it would be hard to work. I was living in faith and in faith I knew that God would listen and step in, if it truly was a need. So I asked him to provide the money for the exhaust and then went to bed.

The next morning an envelope was lying on the front door mat. Someone had obviously delivered it in the night. When I opened it and counted how much we had been blessed with, I was amazed to see that it was £76.32 the exact amount that was needed for the exhaust pipe, not a penny more, not a penny less! We hadn't told anyone about this need, but obviously God had and we were so grateful to once again have transport.

The struggles were endless, but God provided and we experienced no end of humbling moments.

As we lived more and more like this, the more we grew in faith. A foundation of faith was being built. This foundation would lead onto even greater things.

### Forget about your own problems

The work at The Door now became more and more intense. It seemed I was on call at all times and found myself drawn into situations that I wasn't properly prepared for. I made several trips to hospital with young people who had attempted suicide. The phone would ring at 2.00am and it would be a Police Officer or Social Worker looking for a young person that had gone missing. I would help those that had been involved in fights, patching them up where I could or taking them to hospital if their injuries were more serious. I would spend numerous hours sitting in Magistrates' Courts supporting young people who had been arrested. I could see another side to these young people and provided character references and reports. For most of them it was a wake-up call and they never committed any offences again.

One particular young person that was struggling with life was Scott (not real name). He had a quiet disposition about him and had struggled to make many friends at school, although he did have two very close friends and he was gradually growing in confidence. His new found confidence had now helped him to find work and life was beginning to feel good for him. However, when a person is in a vulnerable state, it doesn't take much for all of the good feeling and confidence to disappear. In Scott's case it was a major trauma that would upset his state of mind and his fragile emotional balance.

It was around seven in the morning and Scott was making his way to work. He had been fortunate enough to find work close to home, so it wasn't far to travel and Scott enjoyed the early morning walk. The fact that it was mid November and still dark didn't put him off, as life was looking good. His route took him down a dimly lit footpath next to a park and it was here that a dark shadow of a man approached him.

As the person moved closer and the shadow became clearer, Scott looked at the man's face. He had a desperate look in his eyes and he was close enough to identify the smell of alcohol on his breath. The unknown character stopped and demanded, "Give me your money!" Scott refused. He didn't see the blade of the knife, but felt the immediate searing pain as it was thrust into the top of his leg.

Scott started shouting for help, which was

enough to panic the assailant and he ran away. It was a short distance to the hospital and Scott made his way there for help, where the Police were called.

Scott gave a very accurate description of his attacker, but couldn't believe it when just a few days later he saw him again. He followed his attacker with some friends for safety and then reported his presence to the Police.

The man lived near to our coffee bar project and we witnessed the Police arriving to take him in for questioning, though without any evidence or witnesses, the man denied the attack and was released without charge.

Anger, fear and hate surged out of Scott as he wanted justice and without it he would seek revenge. He wanted to fight back, to hurt this man, but it wasn't in his quiet meek nature. Instead each time that he saw the man from a distance, he would 'phase out'. It was as if his mind just switched off as he couldn't cope with the level of stress that he was now under. He would sit and stare, but never respond to anyone talking to him. It was as if he was a shell, alive, but no life. Each time he would return from one of these episodes he would be angry and "want to kill that bloke!"

A doctor confirmed that this is likely to be the

mind's way of protecting him from the traumatic stress, it was a form of post traumatic stress disorder.

The feelings and behaviour continued for months, until eventually Scott decided that he could not live like this any longer. As his friends ran after him to stop him, he found himself at the top of the multi-storey car park. The drop on one side is about seventy feet and in recent years a number of people have jumped from there, bringing their lives to a tragic end. On the other side, the side where Scott now stood, the drop was about thirty feet. With a crowd in pursuit he didn't hesitate to jump and plunged to the hard tarmac surface below.

With no more than bruises and shame, more anger came flooding into him. His friends helped him up, all of them showing concern for his state of mind.

It was a short walk back to our coffee bar and the first that we knew about what had just happened, is when Scott came in; he was angry. The anger was directed at himself as he made comments of, "I wish I was dead!" As he threw himself from the top of the stairs into the basement, he had reached his lowest point and the gravity of the whole situation was acknowledged.

He just sat and talked, he talked so quietly his

voice was barely audible. Now as he talked, he realised that there were people who cared about him. It would take five months from the point of his attack until he returned to work. His 'phasing out' would eventually stop and he would also learn to speak more loudly than he had ever previously been able to speak. I would meet with him regularly to talk through his feelings, help him to set goals that would develop his confidence and teach him how to project and express himself more clearly. Slowly his life returned. Slowly the desire to live was restored. He had talked and I had listened. This formula has helped to save many like Scott over the years, but I do think that he was the first that I had helped in this way.

After just six months of living by faith and dealing with some of the most serious and unexpected issues that you could imagine, I couldn't handle any more. At the time there was a saying that the average life span for a Christian youth worker was about two years. On average burnout would hit and you could cope no more. I like to think that things have changed since then and that youth workers who are employed in Christian settings are now properly managed, resourced and supported.

It's easy for me to look back now and realise that there was another reason why I was on the edge of burnout. I had worked by faith, but I had also carried out all of my youth work duties and beyond, in my own strength!

For now I felt that God was saying, "You have done enough." He was calling me back out of working for him, living by faith. Six months after standing up in front of the church and telling everyone that God was "calling me", now I was telling them, "God is calling me back out." They had understood when I told them that God had called me, but now many of them struggled to understand why I should be called back from where he had led me?

I believe that we are all like tools in a toolbox. The toolbox is God's toolbox and we are his tools, to be used as and when he chooses to use us. He chose to use me for six months, so that I may learn and become better prepared for what was to come in the future. He put me back for a rest, although it wouldn't be a complete rest. I would continue working coffee bar shifts for another three and a half years before he would call me again.

At the end of this six months 'taster' calling I looked back feeling as if I had failed, but God showed me where the foundations had been laid for the work that lay ahead. He reminded me of those who were alive or out of prison, because I had been there for them and he had also worked a small miracle on my debts, which were now less than when I had stepped out in faith.

# Chapter thirteen

## Highs and lows

My song writing had continued and during my six months of 'taster calling' Dave and I decided that we should produce an album. It was recorded in a day in the basement at The Door. A mobile studio arrived and filled the room. Nowadays it can all be done on one computer.

The album was produced on cassette. It was very low budget and never made any money, as we gave more away than we sold. We called the album 'Poetic Justice' which was the same name that we called ourselves. This may not have sounded very imaginative, but the lyrics were. They were powerful, they were from God! Each track carried a message and that message would change lives.

It was the summer of 1992 when I first met Kimberley (not real name). She came running into the coffee bar on a sunny Saturday afternoon, with two Police Officers chasing her. She couldn't understand why the Police were allowed in and allowed to confront her. To her 'The Door' was a place that was safe, a refuge and a sanctuary, a place to hide and that also included hiding from the Police. It didn't take us long to realise that she was a missing person and the Police were trying to find her for her own safety. She was also panicking because she had been shoplifting. In these early years we saw a very high level of shoplifters and we are convinced that this has now reduced as a result of some of the work that we have done.

The Police took Kimberley away, back to those who had reported her as missing, but for how long?

Over the next few weeks we saw Kimberley on a regular basis. As we started to build a relationship with her, a trust developed. Sadly that trust would lead to Kimberley being led to temptation and her skill and nature as a thief would get the better of her.

My box of albums was now on display in the coffee bar as I was trying to sell them. The sight of the bright yellow cassette caught her eye and in a flash it was in her bag. In her mind she had nothing to lose, she had made plans to run again and this time it would be far enough away that she would not be found!

A week passed and no one saw Kimberley, not even the Police came looking this time. Her absence had not been reported. In the same way the absence of the cassette had gone unnoticed!

As Kimberley walked back into the coffee bar she looked different as I approached to chat to her.

"Hi Kim, we haven't seen you for a while, how's things with you?"

"Yeah, uh... I've been to Cornwall." This was over two hundred miles away.
"Cornwall? What were you doing in Cornwall?" Were you on holiday?"
"No I ran away again, needed to get some space to sort my head out."
"And did you? Sort your head out?"
"Yeah, I need to stop nicking stuff and start to behave and I wanna start by giving this back."
She handed me the cassette tape. It was the first that I knew it was missing.
"Oh, uh... how long have you had that?"
"'bout a week."
"Did you listen to it?"
"Y – e – s," came the long drawn out reply.
"What did you think?"

Then came the story. "I sat on top of a cliff over-looking the sea. I had my Walkman (cassette player) with me and popped the tape in. What I heard in the headphones spoke to me. God spoke to me and I gave my life to Jesus. I want to give the tape back to you now and say sorry."

I smiled as I said, "You can keep it or give it to someone else who might need it."

Kimberley never did say why she was sitting on the top of the cliff. She may have just been admiring the view, but the fact that she was running away again could have meant that she was going to run off the cliff. I didn't ask any more, I didn't have to.

* * * *

Kimberley was not the first to find Jesus through the work that we were doing at 'The Door'. The first fruit came just four months after opening. We had met Joe (not real name) on the first day of opening, though with so many young people on that first day, we never really remembered him. He didn't stand out in the crowd, but to God he was someone special.

Joe told us that when we met him, he was on the streets of Stroud entertaining himself and his friends by gluing coins to the pavement, then watching unsuspecting members of the public try to pick them up. He was seventeen years old and enjoyed an element of fun in his life. His life had not been entirely happy, as his parents had divorced when he was just fourteen years old.

Joe was also one of the two close friends that Scott had and was almost certainly amongst the crowd that had chased after him, just before he jumped from the multi-storey car park. This may have caused Joe to start thinking more about life and death, the age old question of, "what happens after death?"

He would talk to us quite openly about his life, the things that he had done and explain that he felt as if something was missing.

It was December 31$^{st}$ 1991, New Year's Eve. Joe was getting ready to embark upon a New Year, but little did he know that it was also going to be a new life.

Like most towns, Stroud would traditionally see a gathering of revellers that form a crowd around the vicinity of the town clock. Joe was amongst the crowd. As the time approached midnight, the throng of the crowd grew and as usual a few scuffles would breakout. Alcohol-fuelled fights were seen as a regular occurrence during this night of the year and Police were on standby. Joe was normally a quiet gentle type, but alcohol can transform a person, causing them to react differently.

The crowd was rapidly becoming out of control. Joe felt a knock on the back of his head. Someone had hit him. He didn't know who it was, it didn't matter, he just turned and immediately punched the first person he saw. As his fist made contact with the unknown person, his brain went into meltdown at the realisation that his target was a Policeman. Suddenly his world was spinning as in an instant Joe found himself restrained. In his head he was questioning, "How did this happen?" His question of the situation had a repentant nature to it. Now almost as quickly as he had been restrained, he was being released. I like to think that Jesus intervened and said, "Let go, I've paid the price for his wrong doing, leave him with me and I'll take care of him!"

In those early days at The Door, one of our volunteers was allowed to live in the flat upstairs. Joe knew that if he went there he would find peace and sanctuary. He spent the night sleeping in the Drop-In (something that we wouldn't allow today). As he awoke the next morning he reflected on the events of the previous evening and of his life. He had known that something was missing and now he recognised what it was. He had heard the Gospel message and he knew that Jesus had paid the price for him. The price of life over death! He was alone, but God was with him, then as he sat and opened up his heart, God came in and filled it. It was New Year's Day 1992 and Joe was a new creation! We previously had many conversations with him and planted the seeds of truth, God's truth, but it was the Holy Spirit that had brought Joe to the point of realisation and revelation. Everything that he had heard about Jesus was true and real!

Three months later Joe was baptised in a river that runs through a meadow. This place was special, as it was where he had played when he was a child. Now he was a child again, a child of

God.

* * * *

One of the things that attracted me to youth work was the energy and liveliness that is associated with young people. That energy can help to keep us young. Then occasionally we meet someone with no energy for life. Lizzie was such a person.

In that first year of opening she would call in for a drink and a chat, she always had a support worker with her and always talked about her unhappy life. She lived in a children's home, had no family and felt as if everyone was against her. At some point during every conversation she would talk about killing herself. The support worker would smile and raise an eyebrow as if to say, "We've heard this all before". The cuts on her arms, though, told a different story. Each cut neatly in line with the one next to it. It was a form of order in a life full of chaos. Each single cut shouted out, "I am being serious! Why won't anyone listen to me?"

I slowly lost count of the number of conversations that I had with Lizzie, but I was always pleased to see her and to listen, but it seemed that she needed more. The last time that I saw Lizzie she was describing how she was going to kill herself. Two days later she was found hanging from her stairs. The rope around her neck had brought an end to her tragic life!

Now twenty two years later I still question, "did I do enough? Did anyone do enough?" Lizzie was the first young person who I had worked with, supported and tried to help, who was now dead! There would be many more.

By the time the project had been running for ten years, I had counted twenty five young people who had died. Some died in car accidents, others from drug overdoses and some from natural causes. I would come to realise that although these young people were mainly full of energy, they were also very vulnerable, precious and in need of protection. After ten years of counting I would stop, as I would hear God speak to me saying, "Count the ones that you save, not the ones that you lose." Others have died since, but I don't count any more. Some of their stories will be found further on in this book.

There would be many dark moments, but in that darkness, the Golden Thread of God would be ever present!

The next two songs that you are about to read were written in 1991. 'What a Mess' was inspired by the state of the whole world, whilst 'What's going on?' was written in about five minutes one evening after returning home and the frustrations of the day were getting to me.

This was how God led me to be released from the tension that was building up.


### *What a mess!*

*The progress of the nation,*
*destroying God's creation,*
*All around the World,*
*it's just the same old situation.*
*We fight for right we fight for peace*
*and for this generation,*
*Don't give me deprivation*
*what we need is revelation, c'mon!*


*Jus' take a look at the World*
*an see jus' what it's got,*
*All work no play school every day, it hasn't got a lot!*
*This World which we live in, is in a bad old way,*
*All war an fights, famine and plights, look like they're*
*here to stay! Here we go now*


*Chorus:*
*Oh what a mess! This World which we live in,*
*Couldn't care less it's a World without love.*
*Oh what a mess! This World which we live in,*
*Couldn't care less it's a World without love!*


*Let's make this World a better,*
*place in which to live,*
*Recycle this, recycle that,*
*we'll take the things you give.*
*The people of this World*

179

*all think they know the way,*
*But there are some, you may be one*
*that could be led astray!*

*Chorus*

*Now the programmes on the TV and*
*the things that we all read,*
*They change your view of what you do,*
*they plant an evil seed.*
*Like Teenage Mutant Heroes,*
*what a bunch of weirdos,*
*They smell they're green, they look obscene,*
*they're nothing like my hero.*

*Chorus*

*Well if you think you've found the answer,*
*of how to make the World right,*
*Just think again now who's to blame?*
*Will you blame anyone you like?*
*The problem lies in all of us and*
*it eats you from within,*
*The problem then is S.I.N. or call it plain old sin!*

*Chorus*

\*\*\*\*\*

### __What's going on?__
*Feeling tense, feeling angry when I'm feeling low.*
*Feeling down, feeling fed up*
*with the whole of the show!*

*All the bad, all the wrong,*
*all the guilt and all the shame.*
*People dying, people lying,*
*people causing people pain!*
*After all the violence, a World full of silence.*
*No one knows and no one tells*
*in a World of defiance!*

*Chorus:*
*What is it?  What's going on?*
*What is it?  What's going on?*
*What is it?  What's going on?*
*What is it?  What's going on?*

*Smoking dope and popping pills*
*it's just a way of life.*
*A pocket full of money on a pushing parasite!*
*Smoking dope and popping pills*
*it's just a way of life.*
*A pocket full of money on a pushing parasite!*
*An alcoholic teenager is more and more the norm.*
*At the latest victim's funeral*
*two hundred people mourn.*
*How many more will have to die before they realise?*
*They burn their hands when they play with fire when*
*will they realise?*
*Will they realise?*
*Chorus*

*Now this is what I do when I'm feeling low and angry*
*with the system.*
*I turn to my God, get down on my knees and pray*

181

*Lord give me wisdom!*
*I pray Lord give me wisdom!*
*I praise my Lord that he answers my prayers and fills*
*me with his peace.*
*Thank you Lord for your love, joy and strength and*
*your miracles that never cease!*
*Your miracles that never cease!*
*Miracles that never cease!*
*Chorus*

# Chapter Fourteen

### A time to say "Goodbye"

During 1992 my mum started to come to Minchinhampton Christian Fellowship with us. She enjoyed the vibrancy and the family feeling, the place had an exciting buzz of expectancy. She felt comfortable and of course she enjoyed watching me, leading worship and leading young people.

Her enthusiasm for church was now growing and enthusiasm is an infectious thing. It didn't take long before my dad was also coming along every-so-often on a Sunday morning. He also started to visit the local Catholic Church, as this is what he had grown up with. This provided him with the familiarity of what he knew, but something it seemed was missing. At Minchinhampton he was developing friendships and relationships, as people would genuinely ask after him. He found socialising easy, with a natural charisma about him, the Irish charm that could connect with most people.

My relationship with my dad had now become close. The childhood and teenage years were now long behind us. He had been sober for sixteen years and during this time a deep love for each other had grown.

No matter where I would be working on a Friday afternoon, my dad would finish his work early just so that he could visit me and admire what I was doing. He would pretend to inspect my work on the building that I was working on and I began to look forward to his Friday afternoon visits. In fact I longed for them and on reflection I now liken this to the prodigal son in The Bible yearning to see his father again.

Bad health was slowly taking a hold on my dad. When he was in his early fifties he had undergone a heart by-pass operation and we knew that angina still affected him. Every-so-often he would have to stop what he was doing and put a small tablet under his tongue. This had become quite normal and as is often the case, with normality comes lack of concern. It was just another angina attack, we had seen so many and everything would be ok.

During a Sunday morning service at the Catholic Church dad had a very bad angina attack. If you were not used to them they could look quite scary, but he might as well have been invisible. Nobody noticed or if they did, they just ignored him. He staggered towards the door and eventually one concerned lady asked if he was all right. When he recovered he left, then later commented during the week that no-one had contacted him to enquire about his health. He also said that if he had had an attack at

185

Minchinhampton Christian Fellowship, he would have immediately been given help, prayer too if he wanted it and someone would have checked that he was O.K. later in the week. He was beginning to notice some differences. He also started to play worship music in his car and even played some on his harmonica.

The more he fellowshipped at Minchinhampton, the more he realised that there is a Jesus who wants a personal relationship with us. He was meeting people who could testify to such a relationship. He was seeing a new way. He had been blinded by religion for his whole life and now he had his eyes opened to relationship. He never asked many questions, as his way of learning was to watch and learn. The way that we act is very powerful and therefore very important! My dad would comment about the comparison of people that he had met at the Catholic Church and those who he now grew closer to. One experience was cold and unwelcoming, whilst the other was warm and friendly, but most of all God was slowly revealing his truth through his people.

None of us really realised how badly his health was deteriorating and now at the start of the New Year, he returned to work after a two week Christmas break. January 1993 was a cold winter and dad was working outside. He loved to be outside working with his hands and this time he was building a Cotswold dry-stone wall. A week after returning to work he was taken ill and what started as influenza quickly turned into pneumonia. Now with his strength fading rapidly, he was rushed into hospital, where he would be in good hands.

He started to recover slowly and things were looking up. The medical staff would look after him and before long he would be back home... how wrong we were.

On the Sunday before he died mum called my brother Chris and asked for a lift to the hospital. Dad had developed a kidney infection and it was a touch-and-go situation. He was in a bad way, though we were not told at this stage quite how serious it was. Therefore it was just Chris and mum who went. Later Chris told me that he thought dad was going to die right there in front of him, but he made a remarkable recovery.

Three days later I went to visit him. He looked tired, but seemed to be well. I stayed for an hour or so, chatting about life, family and work. It was an everyday conversation and then out of the blue he says, "I've seen the light".

My ears pricked up, "What do you mean by that dad? I believe that Jesus is the Light. Are you telling me that you've found Jesus?"

"Yes," he told me. We talked about how he was feeling about that and joked about how long it had taken him to realise what was missing in his life. I had never seen him as peaceful as he was now. He had a beaming smile and was almost glowing with a new-found enthusiasm, but it wasn't to last long. The last thing that I did for him was to go to the hospital shop and buy him two cartons of Ribena blackcurrant drink. Now every time that I see a Ribena carton, I am reminded of that night.

As I travelled home I pondered over the conversation. My dad had given his life to Jesus! He was now not just my dad, we were both 'Brothers in Christ', part of God's big family. I had never told him that I loved him, but it wouldn't be long now, now it would be easy!

I arrived home and settled in for the evening. Twenty minutes later the phone rang, dad had died from a massive heart attack just after I had left. I couldn't believe what I was hearing I had only just left him. It couldn't be true. This must be a mistake?

He was sixty four years old and none of us had any idea of just how close to death he was. He could have died on that Sunday night when Chris and mum had been called. God though had other plans, he had kept dad alive so that he could tell me that he had found Jesus. Now less than two hours after telling me the great news he was dead!

Jesus told the story of the vineyard workers. He explained that those who came to work for the last two hours of the day received the same pay as those that had worked all day. Dad had only been a Christian for a few hours, but he would have the same reward as those that had invited Jesus into their lives many years ago.

Doubt can have a tendency to creep in and shortly afterwards I asked God if he could put my mind at rest. I picked up my Bible and was led to Thessalonians 4:13-18, I knew immediately that I had my confirmation of where dad was. I knew that I would see him again one day, as I read:

*Brothers and sisters, we do not want you to be uninformed about those who sleep in death, so that you do not grieve like the rest of mankind, who have no hope. For we believe that Jesus died and rose again and so we believe that God will bring with Jesus those who have fallen asleep in him. According to the Lord's word, we tell you that we who are still alive, who are left until the coming of the Lord, will certainly not precede those who have fallen asleep. For the Lord himself will come down from heaven, with a loud command, with the voice of the archangel and with the trumpet call of God, and the dead in Christ will rise first. After that, we who are still alive and are left will be caught up together with them in the clouds to meet the Lord in the air. And so we will be with the Lord forever. Therefore encourage one another with these words.*

When my dad died, my biggest regret was the fact that I had never told him that I loved him. He did know it, as I knew that he loved me, but sometimes it is important to tell people what they already know. I now encourage anyone who I work with, young and old, to tell their parents that they love them. I am also still learning to do this more myself, none of us will ever get it right, but it is important to work towards it.

Slowly life moves on and we all learn to adjust to our loss. Friday afternoons would never be the same without dad arriving to see what project I was working on. I missed that immediately and I still miss it now!

### Humble pie is hard to swallow
Five months later we eventually found a buyer for our house. They had negotiated us down considerably in price, but at least we could now pay off our debts and start again. It took a few weeks for all of the legal bits and pieces to be done and we were set to move out in August 1993.

We now had to find somewhere to move to, but couldn't find anything. To make matters even worse, we had now become so far behind with our mortgage payments, that the building society told us that we were too high a risk. We would not be offered another mortgage. We therefore had no alternative but to move into rented accommodation; it was as if God was teaching me some new lessons.

I had always looked down on the thought of renting property. My parents had brought me up with the understanding that it is better to have a mortgage and buy a house, rather than live in someone else's and have nothing to show for the money that is spent. Now, moving into rented accommodation was my first lesson in humbling. I had also personally never wanted to buy a house on the new housing estate which had been built near to us. In my head I would think, "That is where all of the losers end up!" Little did I know that after eight months of living in rented, I would also end up on the Manor Village housing estate. My opinion has now been well and truly changed!

It was the day of moving into the rented house and I was the last person to leave Zion House, the house that God had led me to build. The rest of the family had left just half an hour before and I had just thrown the last few final items into the back of my clapped out old pickup (another humbling experience to drive this).

Now I felt angry with God. He had led us to

Zion House and we were losing everything or so it felt. As I sat in the pickup I was shouting out loud with anger, rage was taking over and I didn't care if the neighbours heard me. "GOD WHY HAS THIS HAPPENED? You tell us in The Bible that if we turn to you we will have life in ABUNDANCE (John10:10). **I DON'T CALL THIS ABUNDANT! I'VE LOST EVERYTHING!"**

I kept shouting as I pulled out of the drive and heading down the hill I continued, with the rage building. The journey was only about a two minute drive and I felt like I was going to explode, but as I arrived at my destination I felt a calming peace touch me. God spoke into my heart and said, "You do have life in abundance, if you have Jesus in you he is the abundance, everything else is insignificant. You do have life in ABUNDANCE!"

My view changed instantly as if a download had just been placed straight into my head and my heart. I had been thinking materialistically all of this time, now I had had my eyes opened. I had lost nearly all of my material wealth in order to allow me to have a new outlook and to enable me to value that which cannot be seen more than that which is seen.

The rented house turned out to be a real blessing. It was an old Cotswold stone cottage and it was a little like being on holiday, although having to go to work each day (at least I still had some work).

Heather now decided that she would approach our building society again. There had been a change of manager and the new person told her that we should never have been told that we would never be allowed a mortgage again. The Bible tells us to, "ask and we shall receive." She had asked and once again we were able to step back onto the housing ladder and start again.

Now the second stage of the humbling process arrived as we bought the house and moved onto the Manor Village Estate. Although this house was ours (and the building society's) it was so small, a third of the size of Zion House. It would take some getting used to.

We did what we could to improve it and make it ours. We fitted new central heating, landscaped the garden and decorated throughout. We were starting all over again, but this time with three young children.

Decorating the lounge was the last task and as usual choosing the right colour was a problem. At last, after much debate a colour was picked, but after a first coat came the words, "I don't think I like it" Heather was right of course, it was not as we had expected. Then I had a brainwave, "Let's take the rest of the paint and add it to all of the other paints that we have left over. We added about five other colours, gave it all a very long stir and the colour was perfect. I still keep this picture in my head as God said to me, "You have access to lots of different people. Individually they may not look like much, but blend them together in a team and they will be perfect." Who would have thought that choosing the wrong colour paint would teach me so much about teamwork?

It was teamwork that was now causing the work of The Door Youth Project to develop. The project had been running for over two years. At first we had only taken on a one year lease to see how it would go, then at the end of the first year we had repeated it. We stepped out even more in faith at the end of our second year, as we had now taken on a three year lease. This step would take us to a point of five years and at that point another huge step of faith would be required.

# Chapter Fifteen

### The call back

It continued to be a struggle to find building work and in October 1995, I was earning such a small amount of money it wasn't enough to exist. It was worse than the time that I had had to sell my table to be able to eat, but this time help came in the form of Government funding. We applied for and were awarded Family Income Support. This was a fixed amount of money that would be paid to us each week for a period of six months. (This benefit has since been replaced by the Working Families' Tax Credit).

At the same time work at The Door was becoming more difficult. We had survived for just over four years since opening and the work had been carried out entirely by volunteers. These volunteers were all feeling tired and worn out! Now as we met to discuss the future of the project, the management committee were asked, "What is the future? Where are we going? What are we going to do?"

Option one was to stop everything. With volunteers struggling to keep going, myself included in this, it had to be considered, but it wasn't considered for long.

The only other option was to employ a full-time

project worker. This person would take the reins and drive the project forward. We would then be able to open more hours and the work would start to become more co-ordinated.

The choices for this role were Andy or me, although Andy was not in a situation where he could stop work and so I was asked. The post would commence at the start of January 1996 and I would still have four months of Family Income Support to help me. With that help, I was able to work at a reduced rate of pay for three months.

I was asked if I was willing to take that step of faith and I accepted in a flash. Then after that flash came the doubts, the hesitations and then the "what ifs?" Doubt is the enemy's way of chipping away at faith. I have seen it happen in many projects where doubt has crept in, chipped away and eventually blown faith out of the water. Did I have the faith? I had been called before, my 'taster calling'. Looking back now, it was as if God said, "The previous time was your audition, you were good, but you needed a little more time. Now is the time, this is your 'CALL BACK'."

I asked, "What can I do this time that will help me? How can I be better?"

God reminded me, "Don't do things in your own

strength and trust in me. Yes my Word says that you can do all things, but it doesn't say that you WILL do all things. Whatever your hand finds to do, do it with ALL of your might, but remember to leave room for my JOY. The JOY of the Lord is your STRENGTH. Be filled with my joy and be filled with my STRENGTH."

These words, these scriptures have carried me through not just the six months of my previous audition, but for the last eighteen years. Those years have been years of faith without which we would have nothing.

I stepped into this full-time role with just three months funding and guess what, we still have only three months funding. There have been times when we have had up to six months, but generally it is always around the three month period. We exist like this, we exist in faith. Sometimes when I tell people this they are surprised. "Why are you surprised?" I ask, "If we had three years' funding, where is the faith in that?" Not that God can't provide three years' funding, he just chooses not to.

As we have grown so too have our financial needs. In the first year we needed less than £6,000 to exist, but now twenty three years later and with a team of staff that has increased to twenty-five, we need over £400,000 every year in order to survive. Our needs are now over sixty times more than when we first started, but God still provides all that we need.

So, if my short trial or 'taster calling' was like an audition, here I am now on the 'Main Stage' and I had to make this thing work. I had learnt from my previous experience and this time it would be different, Jesus would be at the centre of everything that I did. I would ask him to show me his way.

My job title was 'Project Co-ordinator'. This rather ambiguous title really means 'General Dogsbody', but I was prepared to do whatever God showed me and led me to do.

Sitting in the upstairs room of the project, the first thing that I noticed was how cold it was. It was January and we had no central heating. There was a small electric heater which Di Rowe had introduced to keep her clients warm, but I couldn't dream of using that. We didn't have money for heating, so I kept my coat and many layers on, but still I shivered as I sat at my second hand desk, with my second hand typewriter. Along with a small pack of paper and a handful of envelopes, this was the extent of my resources, this was the office. Now I had to source and secure more money. Yes, I had the incentive that I could be out of a job in three months, but the bigger incentive was that the project could be closed in three months. The needs of the project and the young people who we support have always been greater than my own personal needs and they still are today.

It didn't take long before people started asking the question of, "What do you do all day?" This question would just make me work even harder, as they couldn't see what was going on behind the scenes and that foundation stones were being laid.

The coffee bar was now open every day after school and I worked every shift with a volunteer. We now also suddenly had more volunteers, once again highlighting that God does supply all of our needs. The continuity now improved greatly and instead of just opening and being there, we were now far more proactive in engaging young people. A programme of issue-based work was now planned and delivered to educate young people informally and to focus on the specific needs that were highlighted. We did this mainly through fun games and discussion. Young people were learning, but not as they did at school and they had a choice to attend or not.

It wasn't until later when I did my youth work training that I discovered that informal education and voluntary participation were two of the four principles of youth work. I just naturally started to work in this way. I also now know that the other two principles are to provide equality of opportunity and empowerment. These four principles have been woven through everything that I have done in youth work, just like the Golden Thread of God being woven through my life.

I quickly filled my time. Mornings were spent trying to find money and developing projects. As a need became highlighted, I would look at how we could best meet that need. I had drawn up a mission statement which said, "We exist to seek, identify and meet the changing needs of young people." The seeking and identifying part was easy, as I only had to ask young people and observe. The hardest bit then, and still is, is how can we best meet the need? If money was no object we would never have to ask that question, it would never be a problem, but it is so frustrating when you know what needs to be done and can't do it because of the cost.

## Y.U.P.I.S

The counselling service headed up by Di Rowe was still running and therefore meeting the needs of those with emotional issues. Now a new need was being recognised. Many of the young people that I was building relationships with were struggling to find work. How could I help?

I had employed many people in my building business and it would be these practical skills that I would now fall back on. Looking around the building I could identify endless maintenance tasks or projects that needed doing. Combined with the nagging question from people asking what I did with my time, a new idea was emerging. If I could give an opportunity for these young people to volunteer with practical jobs around the project, they could include this on a C.V. I thought to myself that it's got to look better than just saying that you are unemployed or doing nothing, when looking for work.

It was a two-way incentive, it helped us and it helped them. The Young Unemployed Persons Incentive Scheme was given birth in 1996; YUPIS for short and it was an immediate success. The first two that participated found work within a month. It was a very random and organic project. If there was someone that needed something to do, I would dream up a project and spend two or three mornings each week working with them. It was very informal, no timetable and very little planning. I believe that it was this spontaneity and availability that allowed the young people to feel valued and one of the key reasons why it worked.

### Bent finger part two
You will recall that in chapter nine I had a lot of prayer for my bent finger and God had healed the end, allowing it to move. You will also remember that in chapter twelve, in 1992 I was working with a group of primary school children

in a local youth club. This was the Latch Key Kids' Club. These children were all very interested to know about my bent finger and I would always be glad to talk to them about how my injury had happened, but never told them about how God had partially healed it. If I was playing them at pool for example, one would eventually ask, "Why do you bend your finger like that?" Two such people were Lucy and Shelley. They were seven or eight years old in 1992 and young people can change considerably in the space of four years. Now here they were walking into the coffee bar, though they didn't recognise me and I had failed to recognise them. They were both now twelve years old.

We chatted about any old nonsense, anything that came to mind, it was a way of getting to know people if it was their first time to The Door. It wasn't long before one of them suddenly shouted out as if they were welcoming an old friend, "hey I know you, you're that bloke with the bent finger!"

They told me where we had met and then I remembered them. The conversation then took on a whole new dimension. I had known these two for just six months and it was four years ago, but the memories now came flooding back. The relationship picked up where it had been dropped all of those years ago and God spoke into my heart, "Now you know why I didn't completely heal it. Your finger will be a talking point for many."

I have long lost count of how many conversations I have had about my finger. Sometimes I tell people that God partially healed it and at other times I don't. It's really a matter of who I am talking to and the circumstances. One thing that I do know though, I am so privileged to know why God chose not to fully heal me.

That first year of being full-time, the first paid person at The Door, was unbelievably difficult. If difficulty could be measured, this was now much harder than my 'Audition Calling'. Now though, I wasn't trying to do it all in my own strength, God was in it with me, because I had invited him in. I had realised that I couldn't do it without him and this time was going to be different!

The rest of this chapter contains three stories that happened during my first year of paid work. There were many similar stories that I experienced and I am sure that others have experienced similar things in other parts of the country. I wrote these stories down in 1996 and now looking back, I feel that I have learnt from each one and even more so, others have learnt from my experiences.

# Carol

I will often say that our greatest outcome is the fact that some young people are alive today who may not otherwise have been. If we hadn't been there to help and support them, some of them could quite simply be dead. This became so much the case at one point that, in answer to the question of, "what do you do for a job?" I would simply answer, "I save lives."

The person would then make the assumption of, "Oh, you're a doctor," but I would simply say, "no I am youth worker."

In 1996 we were constantly helping drunken teenagers and particularly on a Friday evening. It was a common sight to see a young person staggering around the streets and we quickly adopted a policy that said, "if we see you drinking outside our premises you will not be allowed in." Another rule stated that if you came in drunk and started to cause problems, you would be asked to leave. The one exception to these previous two rules was when the person was so badly intoxicated, they became a casualty or they were in need of somewhere safe to sit and sober up.

The worse incident of alcohol poisoning that I have ever been involved in happened so fast! Carol had taken a large bottle of gin from her parents' drink cabinet. She had passed the bottle around her group of friends, but many of them had declined the drink as they sipped and said that they didn't like it. Now her friends all wanted to come into the coffee bar and Carol had three options. Number one: she could hide the bottle outside somewhere, but there was a risk that others may find it. Number two: she could hide it in her bag, but staff may find it and confiscate it. Number three: just drink it all as fast as possible! She chose number three and poured the best part of a bottle into her stomach as fast as she could.

She walked in and said hello, but I instantly realised that something didn't seem right. She walked to the toilet and I asked Di Rowe to check that she was O.K., but by the time Di had arrived at the toilet, Carol had already collapsed. Her legs could no longer support her weight, though she was still conscious. As Di tried to help her up from the floor she reacted violently. In no time at all she had Di's thumb in her mouth and was biting down as hard as she could, before she eventually passed out.

We were used to phoning for ambulances or parents to come and collect inebriated teenagers but this was the most serious. Her breathing was shallow; pulse was weak, she was paralytic and unconscious. She was rushed into the ambulance on a stretcher and left almost immediately with blue lights flashing and sirens blasting.

We had done all that we could to help her, now to find her parents and to inform them. They weren't home but a friend of Carol's then told us that her parents are always at a certain local bar on a Friday night. I ran to the bar and upon making a few enquiries found them and broke the news about their daughter.

Upon arrival at Gloucester Royal Hospital, Carol had the contents of her stomach pumped out. She stayed until she was fit enough to be taken home by her thankful parents.

The headline of the local newspaper later that week read, "13 year old girl found drunk." The story read that the police had found her slumped in a shop doorway. The police had kept our name out of it in order to protect us. The truth though is that we had quite possibly saved her life!

We took a huge advantage of this incident and did a vast amount of follow-up educational work around the dangers of alcohol. As a result we did see a massive drop in the number of serious cases. The problems with alcohol would never really go away, but we have never since seen such a severe case of alcohol poisoning.

## Lenny

Lenny was twenty-seven years old (yes I know
that is older than 25, the age that we now work
up to at The Door) when he accepted Jesus as his
Lord and Saviour. For many years prison had
been his security, but now whilst on his way to
his friend's baptism, God touched him and
revealed his truth to him and there was one extra
that went through the waters of baptism that day.
A happy day, a joyous occasion, but it was to be
short-lived.

Lenny was living in a centre for recovering
addicts and whilst he was there, he broke the
house rules and found himself thrown out to live
in a hotel which was full of addicts, where heroin
was being used on a daily basis. For Lenny the
slippery slope was a fast one, the temptation of
the heroin too great. He quickly lost contact
with all Christian friends, apart from the times
that he would bump into people on the street and
he would explain to them that he had been ill,
with a touch of the 'flu. That was the reason he
said why he didn't look too well and why he had
lost so much weight. The truth though was a
different story!

During February 1997 I met Lenny on one of
those occasions on the street. This time he
seemed more desperate than usual with an
additional problem, the threat of becoming
homeless again. He asked me if I could help

him, but his needs were far greater than anything that I could  help with by myself, so I put him in touch with the local drugs project.

A few weeks later I met him again and this time he was so desperate that he was talking about applying to access treatment for his addiction. We began to work seriously towards this, with mountains of forms to plough through and assessments to attend.

Lenny had also recently committed more crimes in order to feed his habit and the courts were in the process of dealing with him.  It was a race against time; prison or treatment centre.

After taking him to a drug rehabilitation centre in mid Wales he was accepted with certain conditions.  He now had to show that he really did want help by 'cleaning up' and coming off all of the drugs.  He also needed to telephone the centre every week and to clear the charges that were still being dealt with in the courts.

Lenny tried hard to clean up and sometimes he would call in to ask me to pray for him.  This was usually at a time when he particularly needed a 'fix', but he still continued to use in a small way.

The pressure continued for Lenny and one day following a misunderstanding with his probation worker (parole officer) he looked for comfort in a bag of heroin and he forgot to phone the rehab centre. The result was hard to handle, his name was off the waiting list and he had lost his place.

As he telephoned the centre and pleaded with them his world just seemed to fall apart even more than ever before. Several other people also phoned and pleaded on his behalf, but it was no use, rules were rules. Lenny had lost his chance and the Magistrates would be sending him to prison.

During this time of pleading to the rehab there was also a considerable amount of pleading made in prayer and I knew that God was in control.

With only one week to go before Lenny's court appearance for sentencing, I felt that God was leading me to contact a Christian drug rehab centre in South Wales. It was a Friday and the person on the other end of the line, having listened to the situation, told me that if Lenny could get there on the following Tuesday, they would carry out the necessary assessment. There was no hesitating, we drove down on the following Tuesday and Lenny was offered the chance to start treatment on the Friday (the same day that he was due in court for sentencing). Amazingly all of the necessary paperwork and 'red tape' was dealt with in the next two days (it sometimes takes months).

Friday arrived, Lenny's day in court. I had written a letter to the Magistrates explaining how Lenny had been trying to better himself over the months that I had been close to him. Lenny's solicitor also stated that I was willing to take him the rehab centre straight from the court room.

The prosecution stated their case and the Magistrates were considering sending Lenny to prison.

Lenny's solicitor pleaded his case with the Magistrates, whilst the Christians in the court room pleaded their case with God. There was compassion in the court room and Lenny found himself on his way to the rehab that he needed so much, that he had waited so long for and that God had provided.

At this stage of the story you may be thinking that this is the happy ending. It quite easily could have been, but we all have a free will. The sad end to this story is that Lenny arrived back in town on the following Wednesday. After only four days he had walked out and was heading back to his old ways. The thought that "you can lead a horse to water, but you can't make it drink" came to mind. Anger rose up in me. I had been used. Other people had been used and worse still, God had been used. I repented of my anger and I began to realise that there are lessons to be learnt from every chapter of our lives.

This chapter told me that it is God who sets us free. He wants what is best for us but he allows us to choose what we do, giving us a completely free will. We are free to do whatever we want but sometimes in doing so we become captives to the things that we choose.

Lenny walked away a free man but he still had the chains of heroin addiction in his heart.

Lenny soon left Stroud and returned to London, which raised the question, "Would any of us ever see him again?"

Our paths did cross again one evening at a filling station in Stroud, as Lenny was back visiting old friends. He told me that he was still trying to clean up and that he was going to do it. He asked me to forgive him for running away and letting me down. I replied by telling him that he shouldn't let himself down and that he should try not to let God down. That was the last time that I ever saw Lenny.

A few months later I had a phone call from his mum; Lenny had been found dead after a heroin overdose. He had cleaned up but temptation had drawn him back, only this time his body couldn't handle what he had previously become accustomed to and his usual comforting fix had killed him. Whilst cleaning out his flat his mum had stumbled across my name and contact details.

Those same doubting questions then hit me between the eyes again, "Did I do enough? Could I have done any more to help him? Should I have let him go to prison?"

The answer is of course that I did my best, the best that I could do to help him. Lenny had been given another chance so many times. We can't live people's lives for them; we can only point them in the right direction and hope that they make the right choices.

### Jim

Jim had been touched by God at a huge outreach event in Swindon. The truth of Jesus had dawned on him and he went forward for the altar call; but like so many seeds that are sown, some are choked by the weeds and the thorns. Jim continued in his old ways and found himself in trouble again and in prison.

After his release from prison, he found himself in Stroud and walked into The Door coffee bar one Saturday afternoon. Now living in Gloucester he was still awaiting trial for an act of aggression he had committed. He spoke to one of the youth workers on duty that day. He shared about his life and the things that he had done, he mentioned the troubles and explained that God

212

was in his life.

I met Jim later that week and he began to tell me about himself, but I felt that some things weren't adding up. The stories were now slightly different to what had been said at the weekend to another member of the team. I began to realise that he may have a problem with truth, with fact and fantasy and knowing right from wrong.

One day when Jim came in he was crying. He told me that he had just found out that his girlfriend had committed suicide whilst he was in prison. He opened up, telling me that she couldn't live without him, that it was all her fault that he was in prison and that in her distress, she had taken her own life. I listened to him and helped him to calm down, but a few days later he came in extremely distressed again and in tears. It was the day of the funeral and he told us that he wasn't allowed to go. We later found out that his girlfriend was very much alive, she hadn't taken her own life and that the whole story had been a fantasy to help him to cope with some of life's problems. He was amazingly convincing with his story and the truth didn't come out for some time, not until after the following sequence of events.

It was the day of the fantasy funeral, but it felt so real to Jim. He was so worked up about it his anxiety was building towards suicidal thoughts of his own.

"I wasn't supposed to go to the funeral, but I went anyway," he sobbed. His eyes were red from the tears, in an obvious state of upset. Continuing his story, he told me that his girlfriend's best friend had later on turned up at his flat with a knife and the intention of killing him. Something was thrown through the window and he escaped out of the door onto the street. Unable to gather his belongings he just ran for his life.

So here he was now, homeless, suicidal and hunted. It was a fantasy, but it was all so real for Jim. It was a fantasy, but we didn't know it at the time! He begged for help and as he talked I listened. It was at this point that I enlisted the help of one of the counselling team and he took over listening as I went to try to find Jim a bed for the night.

As the rest of the team became aware of Jim's predicament I knew that they were praying and I felt that those prayers would be answered. One telephone call and I was able to book him into a night stop accommodation. This was not a hostel it was the home of a young Christian couple. They were expecting their first baby, but nevertheless they were prepared to take him in for the night and give him breakfast in the morning. There were still a couple of problems, firstly he couldn't arrive until 7.00pm and secondly he didn't know the way. The answer, I decided was to take him home with me, feed him and then take him to the night stop myself. Everything went according to plan and when I dropped him off, he continued his fantasy with his new-found hosts.

The following morning when I collected him he looked happier, but there was still obviously a certain amount of anxiety that was bothering him. From past experience I knew that it would be difficult to find him more permanent accommodation and as I phoned the first number on my list I prayed. Again the prayer was heard and answered as the lady on the other end of the line said "yes", I have a room and a bed available, "come on up and see me." It was a bed and breakfast just five minutes from our coffee bar and the landlady was able to sort out all of the necessary forms for the Benefits Agency. Prayers had been answered, Jim was no longer homeless and from the love that he had been shown he was beginning to realise some self-worth.

I had given Jim a parcel of food and some clothing. He seemed happy, making plans for his future with thoughts of college and a career. Then three days after moving into the bed and breakfast, he disappeared without a word. His landlady called me a week after he had moved in and told me the news. Where was he? What was he doing? Would we ever see him again? He had gone taking the key to his lodgings but had left the food and clothes that I had given him.

We see people, we help them, then we never see them again. The pattern was a familiar one and one that we had become used to. It came as no surprise to hear the news and when this type of news comes you ask yourself, "Why did I bother? I may as well just give up!" Then I would realise that this is quite a natural reaction and think to myself, "I did do all that I could for him. It's just a case of some you win and some you lose!"

We naturally give up, but God never gives up on his children. Five weeks went past and life continued as a group of young people began to decorate the basement of the coffee bar. This was a regular event which allowed them to put their mark of ownership on the place. It was at this time that Jim reappeared as bold as life. He explained that he had been living in Staffordshire with his dad but was now homeless again and sleeping in a night stop hostel in Gloucester. The painting project in the basement made good progress and Jim continued to hang around, watching but not participating.

After a few days I realised why he had been

watching. One Wednesday morning I arrived to find Jim sitting on the doorstep. He asked if he could make a private phone call to his mum. He had no money and asked if he could use the phone in the office. I left him for five minutes as I sorted out the painters who were now arriving to work in the basement. Disappointment struck as I returned to the office. Jim looked smug, guilty and afraid. It didn't take me long to realise why he looked this way. I discovered that four pounds was missing from the coffee bar float that had recently been made up and I knew that he was guilty. I confronted him, but he denied it. So I confronted him again and he admitted taking it and gave it back. The trust that I thought had developed between us was immediately gone. Anger, frustration and disappointment rose inside of me as I suppressed my feelings and remained calm.

"I'm sorry Jim," I explained. "I trusted you and you've blown it! I'm going to have to ask you to leave. You're welcome back at 12 o'clock when the coffee bar opens, but the people that are allowed in before then have to be trusted. I can no longer trust you, I'm sorry."

As he left, the thought struck me that it may be the last time that I see him, as I said to him "see you later."

It was as if nothing had happened. Later that

217

day he returned again asking favours. Any feelings of guilt and remorse had gone. Looking back I realise that it was the fantasy world and the confusion of fact and fiction that must have caused this.

Thursday, the next day, I again arrived to find Jim sitting on the doorstep. We talked for a while, but as the painters arrived to work in the basement, I had to ask him to leave because of the lack of trust. He left quickly, saying that he understood and that he would return later when the coffee bar opened.

He returned later that day nearing closing time and he had with him a new friend – a fresh source of bad influence. He said hello and talked briefly, before Jim asked his new friend if he wanted to see downstairs in the basement. I assumed that he was referring to looking at the new designs that were now on the wall and almost finished, but I later found out that wasn't the case.

As closing time approached I checked the basement was empty of people. Suddenly I was distracted as another young person with a lot of problems came running in. He had just punched his brother and the police were looking for him. He too had a criminal record, was out on police bail and panic was having an effect on him. It was dealt with in a matter of a few minutes, as incidents like this would frequently blow up. They come and go, but this one had distracted me.

It was the following Friday morning that I realised my distraction. I didn't notice that the pay phone was missing from the wall in the coffee bar as I ascended the stairs to enter the office. "Who's been eating chocolate bars and throwing wrappers everywhere," I thought as I discovered the mess. I still didn't realise that a crime had been committed as I settled down to the task of the daily accounts. The takings and the float were missing. They weren't where I had left them and the thought occurred to me that someone was messing around. That thought quickly changed as I discovered that the cash box was missing. The week's takings from a busy summer holiday had gone. That Friday I had intended banking all of the money, as I was set to go on holiday for two weeks at the start of the next day.

How? What? Who? I was dumbstruck. I paused and switched onto automatic pilot. Another problem... solve it! I ran down the flight of stairs into the coffee bar and flew down the next into the basement where I found the open fire escape. The previous evening I had been distracted by a minor incident and the result was now major. I walked through the first door, into the short passage-way and out into the open, rubbing my eyes with disbelief. As I returned back through the passageway I tripped over a black object that was lying on the floor. It was the payphone with screws projecting from its back, indicating that it had been ripped from the wall. Its body was smashed open and the contents gone. The payphone itself was worth about £200 whilst the contents were probably only about £5. This was senseless and the pool table had been given the same treatment, locks ripped off, cash box empty.

I phoned the police and whilst waiting for them to arrive I started to make a list. As I was doing so the horror and disgust of it all hit me! The perpetrators of this crime had sat in the office eating chocolate. Even the hot water urn had been switched on to make a cup of tea, but they hadn't stuck around for one. The automatic pilot in my brain now switched off and everything seemed to hit me at once. It was no longer just another problem to solve, this now felt personal. I felt as if I had been defiled. "Oh Lord! Who could have done such a thing?" I asked and instantly thought of Jim.

I my suspicions of Jim to the police, but they had no evidence and were in no hurry to find him, let alone arrest him.

As the young people started to arrive, they were disgusted – their place, their safe haven had been burgled. Now it was they who felt violated and their suspicions were the same as mine. "Was it Jim?" They asked. I just shook my head, "I don't know, but it's strange that you suspect the same person as me."

Later that day I found Jim and his friend waiting for a bus and asked them to come back to my office where I questioned them. "Don't know anything about it," said Jim as he continued to give his alibi. "It wasn't me," said his friend, "I only knick cars, get £25 for each one!" I phoned the police, but they didn't want to question them, so I had no option but to let them go. Soon there were witnesses that had heard them bragging about the burglary and saw them spending a lot of money but still there was no arrest. There was not really enough evidence.

I went on holiday and was consciously aware that Jim knew where I lived. He also knew that I was on holiday and I wondered if I would be coming home to another break-in. I am glad to say that I didn't and when I arrived home everything was as I had left it. I realised that I couldn't go on carrying these concerns, so I handed it all over to God and I knew that he was in control.

Guilt is a difficult thing to live with and almost six weeks after the burglary Jim arrived one morning. He looked different. His hair was cut differently, but not only that he had lost the redness from his face and had normal, healthy looking flesh tones. His facial muscles seemed more relaxed and at ease. We talked about the break-in. We also talked about the fact that his girlfriend wasn't dead. He admitted that he was messed up and was going through a difficult time back then, but that he had changed.

"You know I didn't ever expect to see you again" I told him. He just nodded and I asked where he was living, "In a Bail Hostel" he told me and he added, "I'm getting my life straightened out." Again we talked about the break-in, "You know there is no real evidence against you and your mate but I still know that you did it. You know that you did it and God knows that you did it. Can you live with it? I asked him.

"No I can't" he replied, "I was involved." He then told me how he had opened the fire escape door that evening just at closing time and that he wanted to tell the police everything.

Whilst waiting for the police to come and arrest him, I explained that our God is a forgiving God and that even though he had to go through the courts and be dealt with by the law of the land, God had already forgiven him on the confession of his sin.

The police came and took him away. He gave a statement and later returned to the coffee bar.

His greatest fear was not facing the police though, it was facing the other young people when they came into the coffee bar later that day. At first they didn't recognise him. He did look totally different. Then when they realised who he was, there was anger that he had dared to return, but when they heard that he had confessed there was respect – respect for him as a person, for who he really was, for the real Jim.

Jim still had a long way to go to get his life straightened out, as I suppose in some respects we all do. We can all learn from the actions of this 16 year old who made a mistake, but saw the error of his ways and asked for forgiveness. We all need to ask for forgiveness occasionally and find it so difficult to do. I have learnt a lot from the actions of this young man; about temptation, trust, forgiveness, guilt and honesty. He regained my respect, the respect of his peers and most of all respect for himself.

Looking at this story seventeen years on, there are many things that we would now do differently. We would now work much more closely with the police, asking them about Jim's girlfriend and the reported suicide and the threat with the knife. I would not now take a person home with me to feed them; that could be done with food from other sources. We now have a far greater awareness of those distracting tactics and our security processes are far tighter than in those early days. We have learnt much and we keep on learning. We may be a target for temptation, but we don't want to be an easy target.

The most important thing that we can all learn from this is the importance and the power of forgiveness, plus the release that we find through the truth.

# Chapter Sixteen

### Changing seasons

Occasionally I will visit other projects. I do this to learn new ideas, but also to help them wherever I can. At times I will ask the question, "Why do you do it like that?" (or something similar). Sometimes I am given the answer, "We have always done it like that."

No method, or in fact no project, should ever be done just because of tradition. The "we have always done it like that" type of attitude can often slow down development. A lot of us though can become set in our ways, but we need to remember that some things have a season and to embrace change can be healthy, even if it is a struggle. This short chapter will look briefly at some of the projects and activities that I ran for a season then stopped, but firstly I will share a little more of my personal life.

Incredibly when I was running my own business, I never knew if I would be able to pay myself each week. Now working for God's business it suddenly felt as if I had security.. Some people may say that to have just three months funding isn't a great deal of security, but it is when it is wrapped up in faith! I now had a regular wage coming in. Yes, it was less than my wage in the building industry, but it was regular. This level of security made us feel as if it was a good time to move house again. None of our previous houses had been for a long season, as we were never really satisfied. It had always been our desire to live in a red-brick Victorian house. God now led us to the perfect property, once again giving us the desire of our hearts. We have been there ever since for over seventeen years. Looking back to the time when we had to sell Zion House, I had been so angry at God. Now we are overjoyed with where he has led us and what he has provided for us. We were no longer in the dark valley of misery and debt, we had been restored. This house has been far more than just a house, it has been our home.

\* \* \* \*

Di Rowe was supporting me in all that I was doing. I had been a builder for so long that I was now struggling to call myself a 'Youth Worker'.

"Have you considered doing some training?" Di asked, "It would help you to adjust and it will be good for you and the project."

I looked at various training options, but kept coming up against obstacles. Gloucestershire County Council seemed to be experiencing various problems around funding for training Youth Workers and there was nothing available. I was about to give up hope when Di showed me an advert in a magazine. It was asking people who were involved in Youth and Community work to contact them as they were offering training with a qualification.

Ironically the course was funded by Swindon Borough Council and I attended an interview at their offices. It was at this interview that I found out that the course was better than anything I had previously looked at. All students were enrolled at Brunel University and the study type was distance learning with regular tutorial meetings, residential courses, assignments and assessments. I could cope with this.

It took me the best part of two years to gain a qualification but when I did finish I was told that the course had now been upgraded to a foundation degree. The road that God had led me on had given me more than I had expected or could ever imagine. Now I was a Youth Worker by name and qualification and that was my season of training.

\* \* \* \*

During 1995, the year before I went to work at The Door full-time, we entered a float into the Stroud Show Carnival. I had been involved in helping to build a few floats in the past, but they had been designed and built in just a couple of days, with not much thought. These floats for The Door would be different. The Carnival would take place every year in July, but our planning started in January. Various young people were involved right at the design and planning stage. Models were sometimes made, but always plenty of sketched out drawings in order to develop ideas. Enthusiasm would grow slowly with people discussing the costumes that they would be wearing on the float. Roles were assigned and each float looked remarkable, the result of a real team effort.

The actual build would start in April and every week this group that had now taken ownership of what was planned would meet to carry out the their designated tasks. Everyone put in 100% effort and their efforts were rewarded with prizes every year, often winning the prize for the best in the Carnival. I still regard these creations as some of the best youth work projects I have ever been involved in.

Each float was also designed with an evangelical purpose; this was not surprising as four out of the five that we built would be based upon one of my own songs. I performed each song live, repeating it at least thirty times as the carnival procession weaved its way through the town. We gained a reputation of being the liveliest and loudest float.

At the peak of the Stroud Show Carnival, over 20,000 people would line the streets to watch as this amazing spectacle passed by. We had a team of volunteers who would hand out flyers which explained the message of the song which, combined with the visual image of the float, left a lasting impression.

The young people talked about it all year long, as the fun and memories lasted, which in turn inspired others and each year the team grew with new members.

We did this for five years and each year there was a powerful message. The Carnival eventually stopped due to health and safety guidelines. People started to lose interest as insurance costs soared, which was strange because during all of the years of the Carnival, no-one had ever been injured. One of our greatest youth work projects had naturally ended. We let go and moved on.

\* \* \* \*

Another thing that we did for five years was to enter runners in the London Marathon. Our first experience of this was in 1996, when a young person approached me and told me that it was his greatest ambition to run in the London Marathon but he didn't know how to get a place. As a charity we applied and were accepted for a 'Golden Bond', which enabled us to enter five runners each year until year 2000.

Participation in this event meant two things, yes we could raise money, but equally important was the fact that we could enable young people to fulfil their dreams. Over the five years we would see at least two young people each year presented with a London Marathon medal.

We decided to make a weekend residential trip out of the event, contacted the Methodist Church in Bethnal Green and used this for overnight accommodation. For some of the young people that we took as supporters, it was their first time in London and it was an experience for some that they would never forget.

As the years went on it became more difficult to raise sponsorship and to find the willing runners. We had enabled twenty-five different people to have the experience of their lives and we had all enjoyed five great weekends in London, but the season came to an end.

\* \* \* \*

My role as a youth worker was to assess the needs of young people and to try to meet those needs. In 1996 Linda was fifteen years old and had a baby. She would regularly visit the coffee bar and tell us that whenever she visited the local mother and baby groups, all of the other mums would look down at her. She was struggling to find somewhere that she could feel comfortable and accepted.

We had only identified this one person as having this need, but thought that there may be others. Teenage pregnancy was not as common as it is now, which is the reason why the older parents shunned her.

We decided to do something just to help this one young mother. Toddlers of Teens Support (TOTS) was launched and was headed up by Rachel Coysh, who later set up a thriving project called 'Tiddlywinks' in the town centre.

TOTS never attracted large numbers, but we never really anticipated that it would. However, those that did come along found the support and friendship that they were seeking. It was a toddler group, but all of the parents were under the age of twenty-five.

This was again another five year project, which came to a natural end as more teenagers were having babies and they all found strength in numbers. They could now attend a main playgroup and not feel ostracised. Society it seemed no longer discriminated against them or judged them. We had played our part for a season, but now this too had ended.

* * * *

During the late nineties I had the privilege to be invited to work in an inclusion unit within a local secondary school. This project was very forward

231

thinking and aimed to keep students that were struggling in certain lessons within the school, rather than excluding them. My role was highly pastoral and I know that I was instrumental as part of a team that helped those young people stay in school and also achieve.

One young person whom I helped very closely one day told me that without the support that he was being given he felt that he would end up in prison or worse still die very young. Both of his parents were heroin addicts and I offered him some of the support that was missing in his life.

It was this young man who made me start to realise that there are many others that we have supported who may not have been alive without that extra encouragement, understanding and support. I too had learnt through working in the inclusion unit, but this season also came to an end.

* * * *

Each of the projects in this chapter all came to an end. They were all like my babies. What would happen beyond them? What would replace them? Would God continue to weave his Golden Thread in my life? It is easy to avoid change and stop moving forward as fear reaches out and holds us back. The Bible tells us that "God has not given us a spirit of fear, but of power, love and a sound mind." (2 Timothy 1:7)

This knowledge has allowed me to move forward, to embrace change, to take a chance and to continue on this walk of faith.

# Chapter Seventeen

## Move on up

At the age of forty years I had been the Project Co-ordinator at The Door for four years and therefore gone way past the then regarded average life span of a Christian youth worker. The project and my work now gained more recognition from other youth workers. Some of these started to ask when I would be moving on. I would often hear the comment, "You need to move on for your career." Perhaps if the project hadn't been moving, I may have then moved on, but the project was far from stagnant.

With the counselling service growing in popularity it highlighted the need for a separate and private entrance. Until now, anyone that was visiting us for counselling had to walk through a potentially crowded coffee bar. This was rather daunting for some, so money was raised to install a new shop front and carry out a complete refit. This did require closing for a couple of months, but the youth work didn't stop. By now there was a growing population of unemployed young people who were keen to have something to do and to help by putting their mark on the place. They would also have more chance of finding paid work if they were busy doing something positive with their time. They were helping us, but we were also helping them.

This was not the easy-to-manage established church youth group that had helped us to set up nine years earlier. This group were unpredictable and often potentially volatile. On the whole though they performed well and took pride in their achievements. When we re-opened they had an all important sense of belonging.

If a person feels like they belong, the chances are they will behave and they are also more likely to eventually believe. If these three mile stones are reversed to believe, behave and belong it would be an almost certain recipe for anarchy. I have sadly seen some projects that have operated like this; they never survive and are very quickly closed down.

The building now looked even more the part, but there was still an uncertainty about the future, as we were still paying rent.

We were now about to take another huge leap of faith. Our journey had started with a step of faith when we first opened. Another step had been taken when it was decided to start employing people in year five. Every day had been a walk of faith and the place that it had now led us to was beyond what we ever could have imagined.

The decision was made to try to buy the building we were operating from. There was so much more that we could be doing to make better use of all of the space but we didn't want to spend any more money on a building which we didn't own. I contacted the landlord and was amazed that he agreed to sell. Not only did he agree, but he was only asking for £60,000.

Reality starts to hit with the thought of, "£60,000. Where would we find that kind of money?" We decided to launch an appeal and called it the 'Squeal Appeal'. The idea was that we asked people to empty their Piggy Banks, asking them for small contributions and make their 'Piggy Squeal' with joy.

It was me that squealed when shortly after the appeal launch, £30,000 dropped through the letter box one morning. It was in the form of an anonymous banker's draft and to this day we still have no idea of who donated it. What we do know is that God had provided it and said, "I have given you half, now all that you have to do is find the rest!"

We found it from a variety of different sources and by the end of our tenth year we had taken the leap of faith and landed with both feet on the ground. Now we could develop the rest of the building.

It wasn't long before news of what we were doing with unemployed young people had spread and we were being asked to join a much bigger training project. The Gloucestershire Newstart Network approached us and we soon became a partner training provider. Our delivery of training soon became more structured, with a timetable of who should be here, when they were with us and what they should be doing.

Some chose to do music, whilst others would learn the skills of woodwork or help out in the office. Whatever subjects were chosen, it was me who would deliver it. If anyone now asked what I did all day, I would often give a look that said, "Do you really want to know?" I had been full-time for four years and it was time to find more help, although that did also mean that I would have to find even more money. Over the years we have grown, slowly, systematically and strategically. We now employ over twenty paid staff, but the growth started with the introduction of the Newstart Network training programme.

Lindy was the first person who signed up to take part in this new and much needed programme. She would come in and help out, mainly with admin tasks, but she would struggle with everything that she was given.

No matter what task she was being asked to do, she would always say that she couldn't do it. These were some of the simplest of tasks and even when she hadn't really tried, she would still say that she couldn't do it. She had absolutely no self belief! At times I would need her to sign a form as evidence that she had been with us and without even thinking about what she was being asked, she would answer, "I can't do it." Her mind had become programmed with this response and she had conditioned her thinking to believe this.

I became frustrated with her lack of belief in herself and one day questioned her, "Why do you always think that you can't do something?"

She replied instantly, "A teacher at school told me that I was a failure. I was in the school hall during lunchtime. It was packed with people and he told me, in front of everyone else. He said, 'Lindy you're a failure, you fail at everything you do and it is likely that you will always be a failure.' That's why I am the way I am, he told me that I would be!"

My response came immediately, "I don't believe that you will always be a failure or in-deed that you are a failure." Then thinking on my feet or perhaps it was God prompting what to say I asked, "If you could talk to this teacher and confront him now, would you like to?"

There was no hesitation as her answer came, "Yes!"

Where would this lead?  Was I building her up to a false hope?  Doubt started to creep in as I made the phone call to the school.  The teacher in question had since been promoted to the position of Deputy Head and I was put through instantly.

I explained the situation and who I had with me. He remembered the incident immediately and knew me from school assemblies.  "Come and see me tomorrow lunchtime, I would like to talk to Lindy."

The next day we arrived as planned and were shown into the deputy head's office.  My mind was now flashing back to the times that I had been in a school office and it brought with it memories of fear and trepidation.

The smile on the teacher's face soon alleviated all fears.  A smile is such a powerful tool.  His attitude was humbling and merciful, as he began to explain his actions.

"When I left school," he said, "I had nothing. No qualifications.  I had failed everything and was a failure.  It wasn't until I joined the Navy that I started to make anything of my life.  I was afraid that you would end up the same as me. How I communicated that to you was wrong and I am sorry.  I am sorry that my actions have actually had the opposite effect than I had intended.  Please accept this explanation and my apology."

It was a short meeting, but in that brief time hope came into Lindy's life.  The look of worry and fear was replaced with a smile and a feeling of happiness, followed by release.

We returned to the office and I suggested that she write something that expressed how she was feeling now.  She responded without question or doubt, picking up a pen and paper, turning her hand to poetry.  Her first poem portrayed a beautiful release from the pain that had been deep within.  Over the following weeks one poem after another flowed out and before long she had written a whole book.  She was no longer a failure - she had succeeded at something in her life.

As is often the case it can take a long time to fully undo the damage in a person's life.  The visit to the school was just the start and it would be another two years before Lindy would have the confidence to move forward into work.

That day did eventually come and it was such a joyful day, at last she believed in herself.  She had confidence, was overflowing with happiness and was certainly not a failure.  She stayed in her job for two years before I was asked to give her a reference for another job.  She was progressing, independent, standing on her own two feet. The two years that were invested into her life had provided a good foundation for her future.

### Empowerment and trust

I have met a number of youth workers who struggle to empower young people. Often there is a lack of trust and a doubt that a young person will do something good enough, unable to meet the workers high standards and fail. It is important not to set young people up to fail, but to trust them with the tasks that they have been empowered into, supervise them from a distance and intervene appropriately when the need arises.

We now empower young people in a variety of different ways, with some responsibility for decision making and supporting others.

In the year 2000 I found myself having to confront two young people who had broken the trust that they had been given. They were working as a pair behind the coffee bar, serving customers and taking their money. It wasn't long before we suspected that they were stealing from the cash register. Takings were suddenly down and our observations told us that there was about five pounds being taken on a daily basis. We watched. We gathered evidence. We confronted. They denied it.

I never directly accused them. I used phrases such us, "We have been closely watching and we are concerned that you may be at risk." After a long conversation, with loving reassurance in every word that I used, they both opened up and admitted that they had indeed been stealing.

Their reluctance to admit to the crime was due to their consideration of the consequences. They thought that they would be thrown out, banned, never to return again or even worse, we might report them to the police and they would be arrested!

What actually happened was the complete opposite. They were forgiven and allowed to continue working behind the bar and handling money. Trust was reinstated! I would regularly ask them how they were coping with the temptations and it didn't take long before they told me that they had both also started to steal from local shops, prior to my intervention with them regarding thieving from us. Now they had both stopped shoplifting and thanked me for the understanding, non-judgemental and forgiving support that they had been given.

The powerful combination of trust, empowerment and forgiveness had enabled them to understand right and wrong and also to become valuable in their own right. That value led to them both becoming employed in local shops. The second chance and the power of forgiveness had transformed them.

## The power of forgiveness

In that same year of 2000, I was talking to a good friend of mine, Roger Spiers. We both had a desire to set up and run a Christian Union type of group in a local school during lunchtimes. Archway School was chosen, as their recent inspection had highlighted that there was a need. A group of Christian teachers would meet weekly to pray about the 'spiritual needs' of the school and the students that they supported and we were invited to join this group.

We could see that there was a huge need, but was there also a want? If we provided something, would anyone bother to come? In order to answer this question we were given permission to carry out a survey amongst the whole school. This was the first large scale survey that we had ever carried out and the results were most interesting.

The majority of young people had questions such as, "Who made God? Why does God allow suffering? What does God look like?"

These are questions that we have been asked again and again over the years. We never really expect these questions to end, but the survey also asked two questions that were most important, "Would you like the opportunity to chat about your questions? Would you attend a lunch-time group called '4U2 CHAT'?"

At least half said that they would like to chat about their questions around God and his existence. This reinforced that there is a whole generation of young people who are hungry for the truth. Only about fifty though had said that they would want to attend a lunchtime group to discuss some of the issues. It was enough though and we launched '4U2 CHAT' which attracted on average about fifteen young people. This may not sound like a huge quantity from a school of almost 1,500 but the quality of what we were providing was high.

Our programme looked at various issues and where God fitted into each of them. Relationships, peer pressure, anger, bullying; we had a different focus each week.

It was the week where we would look at bullying and having been a bully at school, I mentioned to Roger that I would like to explain a little about the reasons behind bullying and what may lead a person to bully someone. He agreed that it would make sense to do that, but that we would also need to balance it with someone who was a victim of bullying. It made sense and so he asked his friend Martin to come and join us.

I spoke first and talked about my home situation, that my life felt out of control and that bullying was a form of taking control. I told them about my own pain and suffering, about my self-harming and my mixed up emotions that had almost caused me to take my own life. It was powerful and they could see that the bully is so very often a victim themselves. I also told them that, as a reformed bully now looking back, I realised that I didn't have many real friends whilst at school. What I had was a number of people who associated with me so that they didn't become a victim, but they weren't really friends. Mark Woodhouse was my only real friend and even when I had shot an arrow into his face, he was still my friend!

When I finished speaking, I knew that their minds had been opened, but I wasn't prepared for what was about to happen.

Martin stood to speak, "I was bullied at school," he said as he began to share his story. He continued with, "I was a victim of bullying, I was one of Brendan's victims!"

I looked at him in horror. I didn't recognise him. I couldn't remember him from school. How many more were there like him?

He talked about the fear, pain and oppression that he had lived with on a daily basis. It sounded similar to my own life. He couldn't control those who were bullying him and I couldn't control what was happening at home. The similarities were uncanny, but I had been one of his perpetrators and just one of many it would seem.

He told the group that the pressure and emotional stress had become so bad, that he too had considered taking his own life. WHACK! A reality check hit me! What had I done? How many others were like Martin?

Before the meeting we had been chatting and I found out that he was married with two children. This wouldn't have been the case if he had taken his own life. My empathy was growing for this man then he said something that was like a lightning bolt. He explained what had saved his life.

He said, "I realised that the only power that I had over those who oppressed me was the power of forgiveness. I learned to forgive the bullies. They continued to bully me and I continued to forgive. Forgiveness won. They stopped. There is power in forgiveness and I forgive Brendan." Needless to say at the end of this I was welling up with tears.

It has taken me a long time to accept Martin's forgiveness. The shame of what I had done to this man was a struggle. He would have to tell me on many more occasions that he had forgiven me before it would eventually sink in. I knew that God had forgiven me, but then that's easy for God, he's almighty and powerful and dishes out forgiveness all of the time. Martin was just a man, but he had learnt the most amazing power that is available to us... the power of forgiveness.

This lunch-time meeting was the most powerful that we ever had with this group.

The story somehow found itself out in the public domain. It was a human interest story and we were soon being contacted by newspapers, radio and TV. We both appeared on the local BBC TV news and I participated on several phone-in programmes organised by BBC 5 Live. However, not one of the media sources would mention the forgiveness angle. They mentioned that we were both Christians and used sensational headlines but the power of forgiveness was carefully omitted.

Interestingly the last newspaper that picked up on the story was the local Stroud News and Journal. When they asked for an interview we agreed on the condition that the whole story was told. They reported on the power of forgiveness and over 20,000 local Stroud people read the story.

I had bullied Martin in 1975 and 25 years later we had come face-to-face. Martin is now the pastor of Stroud Christian Fellowship and in 2014 this is the church that I now attend. Martin is my Pastor, but more than that, he is my friend and there truly is power in forgiveness.

# Chapter Eighteen

### Darkness descends

Much of this chapter is stories about some of the dark and oppressive situations that I have had to face. It contains the story of the darkest, most difficult and depressing situation that I have ever had to face as a youth worker.

As I look at these stories I can't help reflecting that God has always been in these dark places with me. His light shone into the darkness, to show me the way through. A well-known poem can sum all of this up:

### <u>Footprints</u>

*One nighr I dreamed I was walking*
*along the beach with the Lord.*
*Many scenes from my life flashed across the sky.*
*In each scene I noticed footprints in the sand.*
*Sometimes there were two sets of footprints.*
*They other times there were one set of footprints.*
*This bothered me because I noticed*
*that during the low periods of my life,*
*when I was suffering from*
*anguish, sorrow or defeat,*
*I could see only one set of footprints.*

*So I said to the Lord,*
*"You promised me Lord,*

*that if I followed you,*
*You would walk with me always.*
*But I have noticed that during*
*the most trying periods of my life,*
*there have only been one*
*set of footprints in the sand.*
*Why, when I needed you most,*
*you have not been there for me"?*

*The Lord replied,*
*"The times when you have*
*seen only one set of footprints,*
*is when I carried you"!*
**Mary Stevenson**

Inspired by this poem, I wrote a rap version and called it 'Mystified'.

### <u>Mystified</u>
*God moves in a mysterious way... Mystified!*

*Chorus:*
*I am mystified by the way you walk,*
*I am mystified by the way you talk,*
*I am mystified by the things you do*
*I am mystified by your love so true.*

*Sleeping in my bed, a dream inside my head,*
*A dream I do not really understand.*
*I see my feet go walking and you beside me talking,*
*Two pairs of footprints walking in the sand.*

250

*Walking in the sand, walking hand in hand,*
*Walking in the sands of time.*
*Walking hand in hand in the sands of time,*
*Listening to the voice with the words that rhyme.*

*Chorus*

*The footprints in the sand see them side by side,*
*The footprints in the sand they will never die.*
*Joined together in love, with a love that is above.*
*Joined to live and not to die in a love to mystify*

*When the going gets tough,*
*I know that you are there,*
*When the going gets tough,*
*I know you're there to care.*
*When the going gets tough,*
*feel you holding my hand,*
*When the going gets tough,*
*see your feet in the sand.*

*In the struggles of life, the toil and strife,*
*When I'm feeling like there's no one there to care.*
*I reach out for your hand and I look into the sand,*
*I'm all alone, there's just my footprints there,*
*And I despair, where've you gone*
*Lord where've you gone?*
*Where've you gone Lord where've you gone?*

*Chorus*

251

*I pray to my God, I cry to my Lord*
*Don't desert me Father you gave me your word.*
*You left us your spirit to carry us through.*
*The bad times, the sad times, I know that you are true.*

*When I cry to you Lord, I cry from the heart,*
*You answer me saying you will never depart.*
*I know that you are always by my side,*
*I know that you are watching over me.*
*I know that you are always by my side,*
*With a love I know is gonna set me free.*

*Chorus*

*In your troubles and your struggles,*
*when times are hard to hack,*
*Just look a little closer, you'll see you're on my back.*
*When all you see is one set of footprints in the sand,*
*The love of God will carry you*
*and help you understand!*

*I am mystified... I am mystified... I am mystified...*

You may be reading this and thinking, "what do you mean by saying 'his light shined into the darkness'?" The answer to that is simply that prayer has underpinned everything that I have done. The twenty three year existence of The Door Youth Project, my eighteen years of working for the project full-time, the growth and success, they are all the product of prayer. In essence, prayer is the battery that generates the power for the light to shine!

It was during the late 90's that we were out on the streets of Stroud, chatting to young people in the parks and other popular areas that they would gather. Some of the conversations focused on the good news of the Gospel and for that reason we had a group of people back at the project who were praying for us. The arrangement was that they would pray until 10.00pm. We would then be finished and back with them.

The evening went well, it was the summer and we met loads of young people, what's more we had some fantastic conversations. We were seed planting and they were searching for answers about life.

I was teamed up with Andy as a pair and Tony was one of those who we talked to. He had an emptiness in him and was searching for something to fill it. He would hear the Gospel message on this Friday evening, but little did we know that he would be found dead from a drug overdose on the following Wednesday.

We moved from one group to another. It was like Gospel networking. As the evening drew near to an end the small groups were now gathering as one bigger group. They were all showing signs of great interest in the conversations that were taking place.

The church clock struck 10.00pm and although we

knew that the prayer cover would now be lifting, we continued. This group were so interested, so keen, so hungry. Then as the clock finished striking there was an immediate and noticeable change.

It became instantly darker, as if a switch had been thrown! The temperature dropped and a chill was in the air, even though it was summer. The crowd now transformed and the conversation became aggressive and attacking. We knew that our prayer cover had gone, and the protection that it had provided was no more, it was time to leave!

### Leaving our spiritual home
From 1986, the year of our salvation, until 2001 we had been members of Minchinhampton Christian Fellowship. We had learnt a great deal and been blessed more times than we could recall through this group of friends.

The Door Youth Project had been born out of this group. It was like our spiritual home, with the members being as one huge, loving, caring family.

The leadership of this church was abruptly changed, as if over-night the three leaders retired or stepped down and they were replaced by a new chosen three. This new regime of unprepared leadership brought about more changes and their lack of preparation resulted in mistakes being made. These mistakes caused unhappiness and eventually people left. We were some of these people.

A lesson to be learnt here is that anyone, in any form of leadership should make plans for continuation of the work, project or church. If the three new leaders had been properly apprenticed and empowered into their roles, there could have been a completely different outcome.

We were now spiritually homeless! It would be two and a half years of wandering and drifting, searching for the right church. People would tell us, "If you find the perfect church, don't join it as it wouldn't be perfect anymore."

They are of course right, as you will never find the perfect church. We did however in January 2004 drift into Stroud Christian Fellowship. This is the church that Martin led and it was now two years on since our reunion at the 4U2 CHAT lunchtime session.

Less than a month after our first visit, someone gave me a piece of paper on which they had written a word from God. It said that it was time that we stopped drifting and put down an anchor. I had never met this person before and he certainly didn't know our situation, but the word was so right. Nine years on we are still there and still putting down anchors, I also now realise that you need to put down more than one.

It was during our period of drifting that we would

face some of the darkest periods.  It is interesting to look back at how darkness creeps in when there is no anchor holding us.  This first story actually came to light in 2005, but I do believe that a lot of the damage may have been caused during my drifting years.

Stress is an unseen killer and around the time of Easter 2005, I was feeling the stress.  These Easter holidays were a particularly difficult time as a number of young people were drinking alcohol during the daytime and arriving in need of help.  I had now called for ambulances on numerous occasions, but we were now seeing a huge increase in drunken teenagers.

My stress started to manifest itself as physical chest pains, combined with shortness of breath and dizziness.  It was a struggle to even walk up the stairs.  Various appointments and tests later led to a diagnosis of angina.  Angina?  I couldn't believe it.  This is what had killed my dad.

I would now have to take medication for the rest of my life.  As the gravity and the reality of the situation took a hold of me, so too did the depressive feelings.  The darkness started to take a hold, covering my life like a black velvet shroud, heavy and oppressive.

As I talked with other people who had been diagnosed or knew someone with angina, my burden seemed to lift and hope slowly returned. Then with the aid of medication, so did my health. The light was returning and pushing the darkness out.

### The darkest hour

Three years earlier in 2002 I had to cope with the most difficult emotional experience that I have ever had to cope with and it happened when we had no anchor in a local church. I would be constantly assessing the needs and asking the question of what next?

The need to expand our training provision was high and the shop next door had become available. Should we grab it? Should we take another step of faith? Yes, of course!

This new space would provide a new shop selling fair-trade goods, which would allow us to teach retail skills. There would also be a small creative art space and a woodwork room in the basement. These workshops would also be able to produce items that could be sold in order to generate an income.

The project also allowed more young people the chance to learn from participating in the building work that was required in order to refurbish the property. A mixture of decorating, carpentry and plumbing tasks were carried out by a small group who worked tirelessly on an almost daily basis. I taught, they learnt, the building was transformed and so were they. It was as we were working on this and watching the double transformation of the building and the people, that it was decided to call the shop 'Tranzform', based on the book of Romans chapter 12 verse, which says, "we are being transformed by the renewing of our minds."

This new project was injecting new hope and new light into the darkness by removing some of the barriers that prevent young people from moving forward.

The shop was almost complete and the sign overhead was installed on the day that I went on holiday. I received a phone call as I was about to embark on the ferry that the job had been done and the shop would now open when I returned, but another phone call would change everything.

It was the first weekend in August 2002. I had returned from holiday on the Saturday and wanted to make the most of what remained of the weekend. So on the Sunday afternoon I was just setting out for a walk on the canal towpath with Heather, when my mobile phone rang. I thought to myself, "I'm still on holiday, should I answer it?"

I almost wish that I hadn't answered, but I would have received the news at some point anyway and however or whenever this type of news comes it's never good.

The voice on the end of the line told me that it was Jo Barber. I knew her as a reporter for the Citizen (local newspaper). "Hi Jo, how can I help?"

"I just wondered if you have a comment about the young person that died this weekend."

"I don't know what you're talking about, I've been on holiday? Who are you talking about?"

"Jade Blundell, she was stabbed to death by her boyfriend." She went on talking, but it didn't register.

I made no comment, as the shock wave hit and rippled through me. Jade had been one of the main members of the small group that had helped to get the shop ready. During the process of working as part of this team, she had started to realise that she had such a high level of creativity and she had expressed this in various forms of art including music, photography, poetry and rap. She was like a budding flower, just blossoming before having her petals violently ripped off and her beauty destroyed.

Her opportunities had gone, her potential would never be reached as her life had been taken. Not an illness, not an overdose, not suicide or an accident, her life was stolen, crushed in anger!

An argument over money had been building all day

259

with her boyfriend. Upon returning to her boyfriend's house, the rage was at a climax. The Ghurkha knife was used as an ornament over the fireplace, but now it was put to its intended use and the knife penetrated her soft delicate flesh fourteen times before he stopped.

I was honoured to be asked to speak at Jade's funeral. Fighting back the constant stream of tears and squeezing the words out between the sobs, this was emotionally the hardest thing that I have ever had to do.

This was a dark place! We were there for Jade's parents, supporting however we could, but nothing would ever replace their loss.

The 'Tranzform' shop still opened and we dedicated it in memory of Jade. A stained glass window was also made to sit above the entrance to the coffee bar. This was based on a photograph of a daisy, which was one of the last pictures that Jade took. It has a jade and pink (her nickname was Pinky) border. Although The Door project has now moved, the window is still there above the entrance to Fat Toni's Pizzeria.

Twelve years on, I can still find myself crying for Jade. She was seventeen years old when she died, but the memories of her still live on in my head.

This is probably as bad as it can get.

Fred Chance, an old youth worker friend of mine, once said to me, "never lose sight of the reason why you do what you do!"

He is so right, yet it is so easy to become side tracked, distracted and bogged down with things.

I do what I do for various reasons, but one of the reasons is to prevent any more young people like Jade from dying.

The shop struggled to survive, as very few people would walk past and hardly any would go out of their way to find us. The location just wasn't right. So after just two years the shop was closed and the space was more appropriately used as an art room. This art space would now help young people who were struggling with life. Mental health issues had been identified as being on the increase in young people. The new project was named HOPE in Art and launched in 2004.

This project would run for a further eight years before we relocated the whole project to the High Street, giving us a chance to open a proper charity shop still called 'Tranzform' and still dedicated to Jade. Her memory lives on. The move would also expand and rebrand all of our training under the name of HOPE Training. For now though we were making the most of what we had.

**The power of love...**

Our training service was now receiving enquires from many different sources; social workers, teachers, doctors, parents and of course the young people themselves.

Neil arrived to have a look around and to see what we could do for him. He was accompanied by his social worker, who asked if we could help him. The social worker explained that Neil came with a kind of health warning. He could be gentle, loving and friendly one moment, but suddenly change. When the change happened he had been known to threaten staff and throw things through windows. He was labelled as 'potentially violent'.

As the social worker talked, Neil just sat, listened and smiled. His cheeky, grinning smile said one thing, but his eyes were pleading, looking, hoping. I could hear his thoughts crying out, "please help me." He was desperate, as he had been in care since he was three years old. His mother was an addict and couldn't cope. Now at the age of sixteen he was asking for help.

We of course took him and he quickly demonstrated his creativity through photography, film-making, art and woodwork. It was so easy to like him. What was the social worker concerned about? Then we found out.

The subject of art involves using a variety of

different tools and it happened that Neil was using a hammer for a task that he was struggling with. His frustration rapidly grew and the art teacher didn't see the moment when the hammer changed from being a tool and became a weapon. She was first aware of the change and the frustration as she was being threatened. He had switched so quickly.

Aggression and bad language now spewed out of Neil; hammer raised high and threatening to break the art tutor's jaw. It was real and he meant it. This was what we were warned about.

Joan the art tutor was a caring and wise person. She remained calm and talked to him calmly; at the same time she was praying. This was real - no doubt about it.

If Joan had shown fear, Neil would have won. If she defended herself aggressively, he would have become more aggressive. Instead she just showed him love, calmness and acceptance. It worked, Neil calmed down and we never did see that side of him again.

After this incident I met with Joan and she told me that she didn't think that she was cut out for this kind of work. I had to explain to her what she had done and the difference that she had made. It is so easy for self doubt to creep in following this type of incident, but God carried her through and the fear left her.

After two months the social worker asked what we had done to Neil. He was puzzled, "Neil is so different, how have you done what no-one else could do?" He was genuinely inquisitive and I thought back through the previous two months before finally answering.

"I think the main thing is that we have loved him. Loved him for who he is, regardless of his history and baggage. That's probably the main difference."

He agreed and said that Neil had rarely known any love in his life, but now Neil was being transformed by the power of love. Yes, he was learning all-important new skills, which would help him to find work or further training, but his attitude had to change. This change could only happen with love.

After he had been with us for just three months, he was moved from his children's home, where he had grown up. Now he was able to live with foster parents, his first real home.

After a year the transformation was complete and Neil no longer needed our help. He progressed from us onto a college course where he would gain a qualification in media technology.

Neil is a typical example of a young person who was trapped in life unable to move forward, with fear of the future, no hope. The strap line of The Door

264

Youth Project is, 'Unlocking Potential... Opening Opportunity' and for Neil we did just that. We say that we work with ALL young people that come to us and we do give ALL young people a chance in life, but sometimes we have to make the painful decision to stop working with someone.

### Notice the danger signs

At fifteen years old Mark was already over six feet tall and built like an 'All Star' basketball player. His imposing size could instil fear in many that encountered him, but it didn't deter me from giving him a chance and teaching him woodwork.

It was not long though before danger signals were flashing across my mind; something was different about Mark. His posture and body language were odd, but his reaction to slight humour was aggressive. He was constantly on edge, unpredictable, but was he untameable? Discernment kicked in and alarm bells were ringing in my head and after just two weeks of trying to support Mark, I had to accept that occasionally the risk is just too high. He was working with sharp tools and these could easily become weapons.

Giving up on Mark was one of the hardest decisions I have ever made, but I now know that I was absolutely right. Just a few weeks later, someone shouted across the road to Mark. It was a light-hearted humorous comment but Mark took it to heart.

He promptly crossed the road, pulled a screwdriver out of his pocket and casually stabbed the other young person in the neck. Thankfully his victim survived, but Mark went to prison for his actions.

Doubt started to creep into my mind. Could I have prevented this? Could I have educated him and transformed his mind? Thoughts that led me to feel that I had failed Mark, "why did I give up so easily?"

The answer is of course that experience, wisdom and discernment had enabled me to make the right judgement call. Mark was given a chance and the risk was assessed. Both of these things are essential, but when the risk is assessed as too dangerous we need to take appropriate action.

Without trying to over-dramatise the situation, the screwdriver could have been in my neck and I could have been dead. With that thought in my mind, I know that I made the right judgement call.

### What's the point?
The three years of my life from 2002 to 2005 had seen many dark episodes. Jade had been murdered, Neil threatened a teacher with a hammer, Mark had stabbed someone with a screwdriver, I was diagnosed with angina, our shop opened and closed again, plus we were looking for a new church home.

The escalation of stress does often go unnoticed and even though I still stood on that word in the Bible that says, "The joy of the Lord is my strength," there is a limit to how much stress the mind can take.

The point at which stress turns into depression is unknown, but it can and does happen.

I had considered ending my life when I was just fourteen years old and again when I was at the age of thirty. Now at the age of forty-five the same thoughts were returning. Thoughts of, "what is the point in carrying on?" My mind was already making plans of how to end everything. There was no one definable incident that led me to this place and I can't really explain how I arrived at it again, but it was real.

Then, in the darkness, the depths of despair, the depression I noticed something different, something that I had never seen on the previous episodes. I was not alone.

I started to realise that others who were close to me also suffered from what some now referred to as the "Black Dog". One of my friends who didn't know my situation told me that that great man Winston Churchill also suffered with it, but he fought back.

My good friend Di Rowe heard about how I was feeling; no one else knew apart from Heather. I had learnt to wear a mask, to put on my shell and not allow anyone in. Heather did know though and understood how I was feeling, perhaps from experiences of her own?

As a visionary person, I will often describe my feelings and situation in picture form. I explained to Di that I felt as if I was standing on the edge of a cliff, looking down and considering when I should jump. Not "if" I should jump, the decision had already been made and it was only a matter of time.

I can't remember the detail of the conversations, but as I met with Di every week, the picture gradually developed further. The first change was my mindset. I was still standing on the edge of the cliff looking out to sea, but the thought of jumping had already left me. Is this what had happened to Kim all those years ago when she listened to my music looking out to sea, contemplating the drop below her?

My mind changed almost instantly, but it would be a few more weeks before the picture in my mind would change. Gradually each week I moved further from the cliff edge. I was still looking out to sea, but now admiring the magnificence and splendour of the vista, God's creation.

As the weeks passed I imagined a fence in my picture and I was now leaning against it, but again looking out to sea. Di asked me which side of the fence I was on. I told her that I was on the sea side, the dangerous side of the fence, though I was leaning against it, relaxed and peaceful. She asked me if I would like to be on the other side of the fence, where it would be safer. I told her "no", I am happy here, where there is a little risk and a bit of danger but I have the reassurance of the fence.

Since then, I have also allowed my mind to realise that there is a gate in the fence and that if the storm blows in, I can easily pass through the gate and head for cover.

I know that some of this imaginative thinking may sound a little odd to some people, but this ability to picture things such as this has not only saved my life, it has made me the visionary person that I am today.

Interestingly we called our coffee bar project 'The Door' because Jesus said, "I am The Door, if anyone enters through me he shall be saved" (John 10:9). Some versions of the Bible translate this to, "I am the gate..." I am now so thankful to my imaginary fence and especially the gate, but of course for Di who helped me to see this.

\* \* \* \*

Even through these dark years God's Golden Thread was weaving and bringing a glimmer of light and hope. In 2002 we launched the "Undiscovered Youth Talent Contest." The aim of this was to build young people up, by providing them an opportunity with direction and guidance, growing their confidence and motivation through performance art. For some the whole experience of the audition was more than they could cope with, but we would always be constructive with feedback, building them up and encouraging.

Fourteen years on and this contest has seen an endless stream of talent. The story of one young person can really sum up what this project has achieved. He came to us for his first-ever audition, but was so nervous that he had to turn away from us when he sang. His voice was amazing, but he lacked the confidence for the big stage of the final with over four hundred people present. We did however, work with him throughout the year and he took on board what he was being taught. Then when he auditioned again a year later, he had improved so much that he went straight through to the final and we continued to watch him develop and win prizes for the next three years.

We have seen many winners move on into the music and entertainment industry as a career; Nathan Sykes (The Wanted), Mary-Jess Leaverland (world renowned classical artist), Harry Jones (team Danny The Voice UK), Kieran Powell (entertained Olympians & Royal Family). The list goes on and on and the standard that we have seen has been extremely high, but it is those that have been trained through our own studio sessions that really touch my heart. I can see where they have come from, how they have struggled and what they have overcome.

Kizzy had struggled to be accepted by those around her. Family arguments and health issues had made her life difficult but now, through her music, she was a force to be reckoned with. Instead of shouting and arguing with people, she could pour her emotions into song. Gradually a powerful change took place as she realised how much people truly valued and admired her.

Charlene struggled with a speech impediment which would knock her confidence but she still wanted to sing. At nineteen years old she had struggled with more emotional trauma than many of us face in a lifetime, but she was determined to overcome.

I introduced Charlene to vocal shaping exercises that not only improved her vocal ability in singing, it also developed her ability to talk without any impediment.

Both Charlene and Kizzy have stories of their own to tell and I look forward to one day reading theirs.

Aisha also came to us and gained from singing, but there will be more about her in the next chapter.

\* \* \* \*

A final glimmer of hope that I want to share with

271

you in this mainly dark chapter, happened in 2004. We would occasionally be asked if we would take a student on placement from Redcliffe Bible College. These students were preparing for missionary work all over the world and it really is amazing to think that we now have people who have learnt and gained from their experiences with us in all corners of the globe.

Meok was Korean and spoke very little English. She was with us for a two week block placement and it was a real struggle. Sign language and gestures can help so much, but it is not enough.

On her last day I was feeling that I had failed to communicate with her properly. We really could have done with an interpreter, but then something amazing happened. She arrived with two gifts, the first of which was a picture that she had drawn and on the back she had written, "Brendan, you are a Pioneer for God, you will drive forward and others will follow you." Although I already knew this, we all need to hear words of affirmation every so often. What a great gift!

Then she presented me with a small black book, so small that it could fit into the palm of my hand. It was a Korean Promise Bible. Every page was covered in verses from The Bible. On one page it was written in English and on the opposite page in Korean. Now I was able to use this to communicate. I would find a verse that related to what I wanted to tell her and point to it. She could then read it in her own language. We used the Word of God to communicate, relate and understand. That was the last day that I ever saw Meok, she had come to us to learn but I had learnt so much just on that last day. Just when I thought that I had failed her, God intervened and showed me something different.

# Chapter Nineteen

### Prodigy - Aisha's story

I take great peace in knowing that we have positively touched the lives of so many young people. Some have just been brief encounters, though still worthwhile. Others have been for many years where deep relationships have been developed with very deep roots. Aisha is one of those stories.

I first met Aisha when she was just fourteen years old and she quickly became a regular at our daily drop-in sessions. At times she would be waiting on the door step before opening time. Her school was a half an hour bus journey away and if she was staying to the end of the school day, she shouldn't be on the door step at opening time!

I soon started to question her presence at such an early time and she began to talk about how difficult school had been for her. Everything was a struggle, teachers, lessons, learning, other students; she clearly didn't enjoy school. For Aisha, as is often the case of those that struggle in school, instead of support there was ridicule and at times even physical bullying.

Aisha was no exception, she often felt ridiculed by both teachers and students. Her reaction to this was anger, uncontrolled and often physically aggressive!

When she was fifteen years old she asked if she could do some singing in our small music studio. The courage that this must have taken was huge and we really cannot grasp how much of a challenge that must have been for Aisha. She had very little confidence, low self-esteem and was completely de-motivated.

However we had been building a relationship of trust with her for almost a year. She knew that we would not judge her or criticise her ability.

When a negative seed of doubt and condemnation has been poured into a person for many years, it's not surprising that you start to believe it is all true. She was so nervous the first time that she sang that I stood outside the room and listened. After just a short time of singing she started to condemn herself, "That's rubbish," she said, "who am I kidding? I can't sing!"

I couldn't believe what I was hearing. Her voice wasn't perfect but she did have very good quality with great potential. She just didn't believe it.

I questioned her, "Who has told you that you can't sing?" Then she looked at me as if to say, "how do you know people have told me that?"

Her answer was quickly blurted out, "EVERYONE! Everyone that I know tells me that I'm rubbish and shouldn't bother!"

"Well I'm telling you that they're all wrong! You can sing! Further more, you sing really well! If people are telling you anything different to what I am saying, they are either jealous or deaf."

I now had her attention and she was listening carefully to what I was saying. I wondered if this was the first time that she had ever heard any positive words as I continued, "Trust me, if I tell you something, it is true. I will tell you where you are good and where you need to improve, but I will always be honest with you and never lie. You need to know the truth and the truth is that you have a gift, that gift is your voice. You can sing! Now start to believe it." I have since talked to many other young people like this in order for them to start to believe in themselves and to undo the damage that others had inflicted upon them.

Aisha was on the verge of giving up but the straight talking, positive encouragement impacted her as reality hit her. She never said it, but in her head she was thinking, "He's right! I can sing! I'll prove it. I'll show them all."

Singing was only the start of building confidence and self-belief for Aisha. When she sang she would lose herself in another world. This was her escape from the struggles that were going on in her life, but when the singing ended the other problems were still there.

She soon entered our 'Undiscovered Youth Talent Contest' and stepping out onto the stage was perhaps one of the hardest challenges that she had ever faced. With an expectant audience and a judging panel of seven experts from the entertainment industry, she was determined to show everyone how good she was. Now as she sang the emotion was powerfully strong, as it reflected the pain in her life.

Her school life came to an end and she left with no qualifications feeling as if she had failed, but relieved to be free of the oppression that had crushed her spirit and caused her so much anguish.

By the time Aisha was seventeen years old, I had known her for three years. I had supported her through endless upsets and she had developed a deep level of trust with me. She would come to me on countless occasions in tears. There was a small child inside of her, but she struggled to cope with the emotional stresses that were in her life. She wanted to be an adult, a woman, but the child always dominated. Tears always came. Over and over I would listen to one problem after another. Then eventually, one day when the trust was fully established I told her, "I don't know what to say... I think you just need to grow up!"

I would not recommend saying this to just anyone, but I knew that it was right for Aisha, for that moment and so did she.

She looked at me and the tears stopped almost immediately. I could hear the cogs of her brain as she thought once again, "He's right! I can deal with this. I'll prove it. I'll show them all."

Soon after this I had a dream; it was one of the clearest dreams that I have ever had. In it different young people were coming into the coffee bar, dragging suitcases and bags behind them. I recognised the faces of every one of them. Some were entering the building and opening up their bags and pouring out the contents. What was coming out was a mess, but they were unloading. Then in my dream Aisha arrived. She was hugging her case, unable or unwilling to let go. She had a look of fear on her face that said, "Don't touch my case, I need my baggage, I can't open it."

In my dream Jesus spoke and said, "I am the key that opens the case, come to me and I will carry your burden."

I told Aisha about the dream and she listened with interest. Soon afterwards she asked if she could have a mentor (we had launched our mentoring service in 2006). This was another turning point in her life and would now lead to her getting help to access a college course with the right level of support, plus it would inspire her to find a part-time job in a shop. Things were looking up, but still something was missing.

* * * *

In 2008 a national campaign was launched with the aim of bringing HOPE to the nation. Churches across the country became united in HOPE 08.

In Stroud, The Door was the only project that was associated with this cause. We decided to provide a night club themed church setting and called it Club HOPE. In total five events were planned throughout the year. Each event was a two hour session, but with two hours of technical setting up and an hour of stripping down at the end of the evening, even with an army of volunteers, it was very hard work.

During each event a prayer team supported what was happening and lives were being touched. Aisha went to every Club HOPE event that we ran, she was being touched by God and the seeds of the Gospel were being planted.

There was an almost tangible presence - a power in the air, the Holy Spirit was here. Every event had a different focus and the forth one was a Drum 'n' Bass night.

The first three events had attracted mainly young people who were already attending a local church and some who were already Christians, plus a handful of young people from The Door. Now at this event we would see many that we had not previously talked to.

As the evening started there was a clear division of regulars and newcomers, the churched and the un-churched. Slowly the divide closed and God gave me a picture. I saw a long suspension bridge with Christian young people on one side and unbelievers on the other side. The two groups started to cross the bridge and they met in the middle. God said to me, "You have built this bridge, but you have to cross it and meet in the middle. Never expect anyone to cross from the zone of unbelief into my Church, without meeting them on that journey."

We cannot have an attitude of simply, "here we are, come on in if you want to join us!" We do need to meet people where they are at!

Half way through the evening a group of young people who had been working on a social action project called 'The Noise' were to give a cheque presentation, to the work of The Door Youth Project.

As the camera started snapping, remarkably the group of un-churched young people joined the group for the photograph. The divide had closed and they were all now united as one group. I believe that barriers were broken down and seeds were planted on that evening, not to mention that since then some of those who were present have accepted Jesus into their lives.

* * * *

Maybe Aisha had made her way into the middle of the bridge that evening? Although, as far as I am aware, no one crossed right over that bridge in any of the Club HOPE events. No one invited Jesus into their lives, but seeds were sown and bridges were built.

For the following two years I was asked to put the Club HOPE band back together, to provide a time of worship at the end of The Noise weekend in Stroud. During this event, groups of young people had spent the weekend working within the local community, painting walls, digging gardens, litter picking, giving away balloons and generally having great fun together.

The event took place in May and we provided a Club HOPE style of worship for 2009 and 2010. At each of these events, we saw at least two young people invite Jesus into their lives. Aisha made that step in 2010, she was now twenty years old and I had known her for six years. She had been on a journey, but she had crossed that bridge, been met in the middle and now arrived.

As the music played she experienced a new feeling, a new sensation, it was an overwhelming feeling of knowing that she was loved. She had cried out to God and he had responded. She immediately felt different – changed. The suitcase had been unlocked. She had accepted Jesus as the key to the burdens and already the load that she had been carrying was being removed. Rejection had been replaced by acceptance. Her repentance and his response had set her free!

It is important to realise that the step of acceptance is only the first step and every step is followed by another, which is why we refer to it as a 'walk of faith'.

If we look closely every walk of faith has the odd milestone placed along it. Significant steps that when taken will lead us onto the next exciting part of our journey.

* * * *

Heather joined the team at The Door in 2004 as the administrator. Although as the project grew, so too did the administration tasks. It was decided that we should take another step of faith and employ an apprentice to help with the increasing level of work and Aisha applied.

Each of the applicants had been interviewed initially by the college, with three being shortlisted for us to meet. It was exciting to have a choice, but before the interview date, the other two dropped out leaving Aisha as the only choice – God's choice!

We interviewed her and she started work with us in November 2011. She was passionate about giving back to the project that had supported and helped her, but she wasn't really interested in administrative tasks and paperwork was an obvious struggle, as school had also been. The reason why soon became known. It had taken twenty-one years of her life, but now she was told that she was dyslexic and she began to understand why she had struggled at school. Now she understood why she hadn't learnt and why she had been misunderstood.

She did complete her business administration apprenticeship, but it was clearly obvious throughout that she would rather be directly supporting and helping young people. She had a heart to become a youth worker and as I have often said before, God will always give us the desire of our heart.

We never felt that it would be right to take Aisha on as a youth worker without her first gaining more experience in a wider setting. She was disappointed to hear that, but as her apprenticeship with us ended, another opportunity arose.

We work very closely with many other organisations and PSALMS is one of them. This organisation provides a variety of youth and children's projects across the district and they were now looking for a new intake of Interns.

Aisha was accepted and started with PSALMS in September 2012 and also started on the Centre for

Youth Ministries Engage course. I would see her every so often and I could see that she was growing, growing in ability, maturity and in spirit.

Within six months she came back to The Door and joined our team of sessional youth workers and was showing a natural talent to be able to empathise with those in need.

During her teenage years she had been tempted into shoplifting, sought solace in alcohol and even had a few run-ins with the local police. All of this was part of her life experience and all of it was providing her with a knowledge base, equipping her for the work that she was now doing.

Aisha is now a major part of the team at The Door and I feel so privileged to have walked with her on her journey, to see her overcome, to witness her maturing and blossoming, but most of all to see her giving back and taking the project on with the next generation.

## Rosie

I first met Rosie when she was 11 years old. She seemed mature in her attitude for her age and I constantly asked her if she was really age 14.

She was just 12 years old when she came with me on a walk. After walking several miles we sat for a rest on a fallen tree and started to talk about her hopes for the future.

"I think my mum would like it if I became a teacher," she said.

"Is that because your mum is a teacher?" I asked cynically.

"Probably, but I don't think it's for me"

"What is for you?"

"I want to be a youth worker." She said it with such conviction.

I had often heard other young people say that they would like to be a youth worker. Usually this is because they see the youth worker having fun, playing games and generally socialising. They fail to see the struggles associated with the role and the associated paperwork, planning, preparation, reporting, etc.

Rosie was different even at this young age she knew what was involved and what she wanted!

As The Door developed, so did Rosie mature as a person. She was keen to volunteer, helping wherever she could, learning whenever she could, participating in everything that was going.

Rosie was another that had attended every Club HOPE event that we had delivered and a spark had been planted in her heart. As she grew, that spark grew into a flame and she too invited Jesus into her life when she was about 15 years old.

There is an expression that I love, "People don't care about how much you know, until they know how much you care." When I hear this expression I often think of Rosie as she continued to volunteer in such a caring and genuine manner.

It's not surprising then that when she had completed her A levels at the age of 18 she started a University degree in... Yes, you guessed it, youth work. She had come a long way since the day we sat on the fallen tree, but Rosie's focus and determination, combined with the influence of a team of great youth work role models, will guarantee that she will become a superb youth worker.

### Grace

I have appeared on numerous radio programmes and on one occasion I was asked if I could be interviewed at The Door. It was with Richard Atkins from BBC Radio Gloucestershire and he asked if we could also include a young person comment.

We stood outside in the open air; it was one of Richard's techniques for creating an atmosphere. I can't remember any of the questions that Richard asked, but I clearly remember what Grace said – "Before I came to The Door I didn't really feel valued, not by friends or teachers, not even by my family. Then I came here and realised that these people cared about me and valued me."

Richard immediately placed the microphone by my mouth and asked what I thought of that comment. I couldn't speak properly and I cried on radio as I choked the words out, "I never knew that we had had such an effect on Grace's life".

Grace was another that volunteered with us and was a valued member of the team when we launched a weekly detached youth work session on the streets and in the parks of Stroud. She had learnt enough about youth work to encourage her to step out on her journey in a youth work career.

Grace now works as a youth support worker for the Stroud Targeted Support Team. She is now helping others to believe in themselves and to feel valued.

When you throw a rock into a pond the ripples radiate outwards. We impacted the lives of Aisha, Rosie and Grace, but the ripples of our impact are still continuing. What's more, they will never stop, as these three will also be blessed with prodigy of their own.

# Chapter Twenty

### A time to build up

As is the case with anyone's life, many of the stories overlap, intertwine and run parallel to others. Our lives are a continuous, ever expanding, ever increasing tapestry of new challenges, decisions and excitement. In fact every day is a new day and an opportunity to change.

At times I will hear a person say, "I just want it to stay the way that it is." Those that dwell in the past will also be heard to say, "If only we could get back to the way it used to be!"

My life has moved on. The Door Youth Project has moved on and the time will come when I will move on to whatever is the next chapter in my life. First though, let's try to bring the journey so far right up to date, to a conclusion that will hopefully inspire others.

The book of Ecclesiastes talks about "a season for everything... a time to build up and a time to tear down." Looking back over the last twenty-three years, there have been definite times when this has been the case for The Door Youth Project.

Our Toddlers of Teens Support group was in place for a season. During those years it had served a purpose, but we recognised that we had reached a place where it was no longer needed.

The counselling service that was set up by Di Rowe had continued for twelve years until 2003 and was provided purely by volunteers. These volunteers were in training with Teens in Crisis (another Christian organisation) and were working towards a qualification in counselling. Teens in Crisis were specialists in counselling and were gaining contracts to provide a counselling service in various schools. With these contracts came the necessity to employ paid staff and these volunteers were offered these emerging opportunities.

The need for young people who were not in school, to be able to access a free and confidential counselling service still existed and we could still provide the space for this. It was therefore decided that we should enter into a formal partnership agreement with Teens in Crisis, so in 2003 we made that step.

For two years we continued as we were previously. Teens in Crisis delivered counselling from our property, we charged them for room hire as we always had and nothing else really developed. Then after two years we both asked the question, "Is this really a partnership? Is it worth continuing?"

The formal partnership as it was ended, however nothing changed. We continued to provide space to deliver counselling and we continued to charge them for the use of that space. We still provide that same space now in 2014.

We had both learnt something about true partnership through this process. Now, whenever I am considering a partnership, I consider what both we and the other parties are able to bring to the table. I now feel that a true partnership should result in the combined sum of resources being greater than its natural sum. In other words if each organisation brings one skill, service or resource to the mix, the natural sum is two. However, in true partnership the combined force is greater than the natural and one plus one becomes three or more. That's synergy!

Interestingly as the TIC partnership came to an end in 2005, I felt that God was saying, "now is the time to rebuild." This was confirmed as I prayed and was led to the book of Haggai chapter 1 verses 3-6 which read:

"Then the word of the LORD came through the prophet Haggai: "Is it a time for you yourselves to be living in your panelled houses, while this house remains a ruin?"

Now this is what the LORD Almighty says: "Give careful thought to your ways. You have planted much, but harvested little. You eat, but never have enough. You drink, but never have your fill. You put on clothes, but are not warm. You earn wages, only to put them in a purse with holes in it."

The way forward needed to see us increase capacity, capability and sustainability. We needed to assess the needs, identify how we could meet those needs and determine how we were best suited to deliver what was required.

Having severed the TIC partnership, we quickly identified that there was an increasing demand for emotional needs support of a different kind, as most of the issues that we were seeing were not as deep and severe. They didn't require counselling.

Mentoring was becoming a buzz word. It had a growing popularity amongst young people as it was now regarded as 'cool' to have a mentor (it was also helpful). So in 2006 we launched 'The Light at The Door' mentoring service for young people.

Eight years on this service has expanded to include the parents and carers of young people and now provides: school-based mentoring, peer mentors, family support, parenting programmes and of course continues to provide one-to-one mentoring for young people.

The Light at The Door is now regarded as one of the leading family support services within Gloucestershire. The service has come such a long way since the decision to rebuild.

A year later in 2007, it was becoming increasingly apparent that we were running out of space. I quickly lost count of the number of times someone jokingly said, "we need a bigger building!"

26 Gloucester Street was our birth place, with years of memories, my memories. The emotional attachment was massive and God knew that, but he also wanted us to move.

Now I realise that when emotional attachment gets in the way of where God wants us to go, he will often show us an easier, more achievable step towards where he wants us to go and what he wants us to do. This was certainly the case with how we moved from our outgrown building to where we are now.

A large building which was just across the road from our project had stood vacant for some time. It seemed the answer to our space issue, as we would be able to stay where we were and expand into this. It seemed like the perfect answer.

Sitting at my favourite place on the local common, I prayed about the situation. I was led to various verses in the Bible to inspire me and I believed that God wanted me to call for volunteers to walk around the building opposite. If we were to claim this building, we had to do it like Joshua walking around Jericho. We would walk around for seven days and on the seventh day, we would walk around seven times. The number seven was very significant in what God had shown me and I sent out a request for seven volunteers to be at the property at 7.00am for seven days, starting on the $7^{th}$ of July ($7^{th}$ month) 2007.

This is what I felt God was leading me to do and if less than seven people would turn up, I would feel that I had to cancel this whole thing. The seven people would be the confirmation that this is what was needed to be done.

On the morning of $7^{th}$ July, I drove the car into Stroud with Heather by my side. As I arrived I counted, $1 - 2 - 3 - 4 - 5$. "Yes, with the two of us, that's seven!"

Each day the seven of us met at 7.00am and walked around the building in silence as we prayed.

On the seventh day we met and started to walk and pray in silence. There was a powerful presence with us. God was with us! I had confirmation of this presence as a man in his 30's called 'Timmy' approached me.

Timmy always wanted to talk and I had a concern that he would distract from what we were building here. As he approached, I felt God tell me to put my hand up as if to stop him. I never touched Timmy, but as I put my hand up, it was as if he was physically pushed back. The power of God truly was working in what we were doing.

By the time we had completed seven laps a few people were watching from afar, as Bill produced a Ram's Horn Trumpet (Shofar Horn) and blew loudly. The gathering audience may have thought that we were a bunch of weird religious 'nutters'. I doubt whether any knew what we were doing, but none of them asked.

How would we have answered them anyway? Did any of us really know what we were doing? The simple answer is we were being obedient to what God had told us to do!

We thought that this was the building to meet our needs, but it was more like the building to meet God's needs. He needed to motivate us, to stir us up to thinking beyond where we were at. This wasn't the building that he wanted us to go to but it was what we could see and relate to, so God used it.

In faith we negotiated a price for the building, but following a structural survey we realised that it was in such a bad state of repair, we would have to spend too much money on it. This is not to say that we did not have faith that God could provide this money but we have to be good stewards of what we are given and suddenly this didn't feel right.

The thought seed though had been planted, God

had stirred us up and we would find something else!

God had given us the push that we needed and now we launched an appeal. Calling it the PUSH The Door Appeal, we asked people to get behind the project and become PUSH Partners.

These PUSH Partners would commit to donating a regular amount of money, which could be used to pay a mortgage on a new building, if we had enough.

We looked at three more buildings, each one with potential. The first of these was again not quite right, as it was considered to be in the wrong location. We had asked young people in a survey where they would like The Door situated and we were listening to them. Were we listening to God though?

The next property was huge, more than we would need, which would mean that we could rent some of the space out. We made an offer which was not refused. The building was owned by a large corporation and they told us that they would be happy for us to have it at the offer price. Then nothing else happened until we heard that they had sold it to someone else, without telling us.

The next building was in a great location, but not big enough. Once again we found ourselves in a situation of potentially buying a building and spending money on it, for it to not be worth what we had paid in total. We were reminded that we need to be good stewards of money and even more so when it has been donated by others.

There is an expression that I have used on many occasions, "when one door closes another one opens." Nearly three years had passed since the Joshua walk around the original building. Now with the world in economic crisis and the country being declared as in recession, youth services amongst others were being cut. The 'Connexions' service had been situated at the top of the High Street for many years, supporting young people and helping them to move forward in life. Now though, as a result of the cuts, they had closed.

God had led me to this building or at least a small part of it, many years ago when we were looking for workshop space in 2002. On that occasion I had just missed out on the chance for this space, which was about 25% of the whole building. Now though it was the other 75% that was available, with a High Street location, a more visible presence and a chance to set up a shop to raise part of our own income. This property would take almost a year of negotiations and to work through the legal requirements.

The owner didn't want to sell and so we were back in the situation that we had faced when we first started all of those years ago in 1991. We were paying rent, but God had told us to rebuild, so here we were starting over again.

In 2007 we had stepped out in obedience with the Joshua walk. This was followed by almost five years of what now seems like wandering in the wilderness.

A seed has to be planted and propagated before it grows and in February 2012 we were given the keys to our new building.

In faith I had advertised an open evening on $5^{th}$ February at 7.00pm and was given the keys at 5.00pm, just two hours before the event.

I ran around this amazing new space putting notices up to explain what we were going to do with the building. It took me just ten minutes and at the end of it, I felt God say, "this isn't going to be big enough." Now after just two years of being there, we are beginning to say, "we need more space."

Our plan for the first year in this new building was to just settle in and consolidate, but God had other plans. In that first year we saw the number of young people that we engage with increase from 700 to over 1,000. Our training, mentoring and family support services all increased in capacity, with increased service level agreements. Staffing levels had to be increased to meet the rising demand and inevitably so did expenditure, as our turnover rose from around £200k to over £300k.

We had rebuilt! At times it had been painful, tedious and frustrating, but we had done it. We had remained hopeful, faithful and prayerful. It is the power of prayer and the support of others praying, that had brought us to this place. It is that same power that leads us and drives us on now, as we know that, "God will supply all of our needs."

# Chapter Twenty One

## Reaching out with more HOPE

I have previously mentioned that 2008 was the year of HOPE 08 and we provided an opportunity for young people to attend Club HOPE. Not surprising this year was also a year with more difficult struggles.

Our mentoring service for young people was now in its second year and some of the issues that we were now dealing with were some of the most serious. Now six years on we still see situations of the most serious nature, but this next story sums up all that we do and the difference that we have made.

Annie Watkins was now heading up our mentoring service for young people and she found herself supporting three who had established a suicide pact. They had all agreed between them that if one died, the other two would take their own lives. To make matters worse and to increase the risk of death, they were playing very dangerous games such as 'chicken' with trains. We nicknamed them the 'Railway Children' and over time Annie helped each of them to see the danger of what they were doing, to value their lives and to move forward. Each of them found something positive to focus on and work towards. Before Annie had intervened, these three were desperate and depressed, but having someone to talk things over with had saved them.

Others have taken their own lives since, others that perhaps had no-one they could turn to for help, no-one who would listen to them.

At about the same time in 2008, groups of young people in Bridgend in South Wales were taking their own lives, as they too had agreed their own suicide pacts. The difference between Stroud and Bridgend was that in Stroud, these three young people found help through The Door Youth Project. We were there for them. It would most likely have been more like the sad stories that we heard coming from Bridgend, if we hadn't helped.

I know that I say it over and over, but I'll say it again, "there are young people alive today who may not otherwise have been so. This is one of the greatest outcomes that we can achieve."

**More health issues**

2008 was also the year that I was diagnosed with Polycystic Kidney Disease. This hereditary disease can cause raised blood pressure, reduced kidney function, risk of stroke and could even result in the eventual need for a kidney transplant.

As the news of this latest health issue started to sink in, I questioned my ability and my worth. As I prayed about this, God spoke to me once again through his Word and a picture.

First I saw a picture of an apple in a bowl. It had been sitting there for so long that the bottom had started to rot under its own weight.

Then I opened my Bible and started to read in Leviticus chapter 3. It was talking about 'fellowship offerings' and mentioned kidneys four times.

I felt that God was saying, "your kidneys may be rotten, as is half of this apple, but the rest is useful. You are useful. You may not be as fit as you used to be, but I want you and I need you to be wholly available to me!"

I still had a use, a value and my self-worth quickly returned.

### Preparations for the future
I can often liken myself to 'Eeyore', the depressive donkey in Winnie the Pooh. For brief moments, I may find myself in extremely low places, with the thoughts of "nobody loves me" in my mind.

Then I feel as if God reaches down and picks me up. He carries me when times are difficult, just like that 'Footprints' poem (previously mentioned in chapter 18).

If 2008 was designated as the year of 'HOPE', what hope was there for The Door and the future of the project? I went to the Trustees and explained that the project was vulnerable, because I am vulnerable.

It was decided that it was time that I had a deputy, someone who could take some of the ever-increasing workload and eventually take on the succession when I have gone. This step was considered essential if it was to continue beyond my life time.

We placed an advertisement for this new post in the Christian Youth Work Magazine and in September 2008 I received a phone call from Barrie Voyce.

Barrie was still in his final year of a Centre for Youth Ministry BA course in youth work and theology. He explained that he would not be available for nine months, but would it still be worthwhile if he applied?

I told him that I would be willing to wait for the right person, the person that God wants for us. Whilst most of the other students on Barrie's course were seeking work in church settings, Barrie had felt that God was leading him to a different challenge, the challenge of supporting un-churched young people.

The next month in October Barrie came to visit. Whilst I was showing him around he asked how long we had funding for. This, for some people, may be a difficult question to answer as the real questions could be considered to be, "do you have enough to pay me? How secure is my job?"

I told him that nothing is ever guaranteed, that we could usually see about three months ahead, but that we had faith that God provides all of our needs. Later Barrie told me that it was this honesty and faith that had convinced him that this was where God wanted him to be.

In December 2008, Barrie returned with his wife and two children. Would they want to move from Nottingham to a new town, a new job, a new step of faith?

Both Helen and Barrie agreed that they felt that God was drawing them to Stroud and on 1st July 2009 Barrie started work with us. At first he found rented accommodation, but when he announced that he was buying a house in Stroud, I had two thoughts. The first was, "good he is here to stay." The second was, "now we need even more faith, that we can keep paying him, so that he can pay his mortgage!"

It is these often nagging second thoughts that can stir up fear and prevent the step of faith ever being taken, but when we rise up above them, it is then that we see amazing things happen.

Over the years that Barrie has been with us, he has moved from leading one department to the next. Firstly heading up the youth work team and the Drop-In, then the Mentoring and Family Support, now he is managing and developing the HOPE Training Department. He has learnt the intricacies of each department, to the extent that he became the Director of all Operations.

Like me, he has great vision and passion for young people and their families. He is my successor and will eventually lead the whole organisation forward into new and unchartered territory. The thought of that is rather frightening, for both him and myself, but I also realise that it is necessary.

I have seen too many projects die with the death of the founder. I want to see my legacy continue to survive, I want to watch it from a distance and smile as I see it grow. I want to see others continue to nurture the seeds that I have planted, but most of all... I want to know whatever God has planned next for my life. I want to continue to step out in faith and to walk in faith, walking into the next chapter of my life... whatever that may be.

# Chapter Twenty Two

## Climb every mountain

I started my story with my reflective thoughts from childhood and mentioned the Sound of Music. One of my favourite songs from that musical is 'Climb every mountain.'

Something that I haven't mentioned yet is my love for mountains. I didn't climb a mountain until I was 37 years old, which is when I was invited to North Wales for a weekend of walking. That first mountain was 'Tryfan'.

A year later I was taking part in the National Three Peaks challenge, climbing the tallest mountains in Wales, England and Scotland, all within 24 hours. I am pleased to say that I managed all three in 23 hours and 20 minutes. What an experience!

My love for mountains continued to grow and so too did the level of challenge that I would push myself to achieve. I was 41 years old in 2001 and for many years I had wanted to climb Mount Kilimanjaro, Africa's tallest mountain and the tallest free standing mountain in the World. I had wanted to do this in my 40th year but the house that we were living in was in a mess. I had to finish building the new extension and fit the kitchen before I could go. We all need some form of motivation and incentive in life and Kilimanjaro was mine.

The year following 'Kili' I rose to another challenge. The 15 peaks challenge involves climbing the 15 Welsh mountains, all of which are over 3,000 feet above sea level. I did this in three days, unlike some that do it in a breathtaking 24 hours.

I had developed a real passion for mountains, or so I thought. I now say that I enjoy being on top of a mountain, but the climb up is often a hard, difficult struggle. Although the pain of the climb is worth it when greeted by the pleasure of being on top of the mountain, the feeling of success outweighs the pain and the freedom of the top of the world is breathtaking.

I don't wish to bore you with stories about mountains, but needless to say I have now climbed many.

My favourite mountain to climb with people that have never been up a mountain is Sugar Loaf in the Brecon Beacons. I have been there on many occasions with small groups of young people and after a long hard walk, when we are in sight of the summit I stop and sit. I give them the choice to continue to the summit or to give up, taking the easier exit route off the mountain. Not once has anyone ever said that we should give up.

Before starting to walk again (and they are very keen to reach the top) I ask them all to look back at this time, that if they ever feel like giving up with the huge mountains (tasks) that life throws at us, remember that the end is in sight.

I have had to remind myself of this on many occasions and have been supported by the people that I have around me. They have encouraged me in life, just as we encourage each other to press on towards the goal of that mountain summit.

I have so many people to thank for supporting me on my journey through life, but most of all I thank God, for continuing to weave his Golden Thread and I ask with great expectation, "what next?" I don't expect to 'climb every mountain' but I do know that he will show me which one is next.

This book is my story, but it is not my whole story. I have had to make decisions about what to put in and what to take out. I hope that it has given you a 'flavour' of who I really am and most of all has inspired you to climb every mountain that God gives you in life.

When you are writing your own life story it is hard to know where to end. After all, the story of my life is still being written. Every day a new chapter is being played out. One of my most recent chapters was an eight day stay in hospital. My angina had suddenly changed and I found myself waking up with pains in my chest and arms. I knew what it was and suspected what the outcome would be. The medical team put me back together again, fitting three small devices called 'stents' into my arteries, the shock was soon over and normal life restored.

It was just after this time that God placed a picture of a balloon in my mind. The balloon was fully inflated and I asked God why I was seeing this. He said, "this balloon is like your confidence, fully inflated and this is how people see you." Then he said, "but it only takes one small pin prick and it is burst, your resilience is thin and weak. People don't see this; they only see your confidence."

This book may have been a revelation to some people. This last statement may have been especially revealing to some, as I lower my guard and allow people to see me for who I am and what I am. My experiences of life have taught me that honesty, integrity, truth and respect are the four virtues that will bring us success. Richard Branson is well known for quoting this, but long before Mr. Branson made this profound statement Jesus said, "I am the truth and the truth will set you free." (John 14:6 & John 16:13).

We all have a story. Stories are powerful. So I urge you to write yours. Be truthful with your words and honest to yourself, you deserve it.

**Start small… dream big… believe!**

## Song lyrics not previously mentioned

I truly believe that all of my song lyrics are the inspired word of God, given to me over a period of time from the late 80's to the mid 90's. These songs all have a powerful message, as Kimberley found out (page 171)

These songs were used in school assemblies (mainly at Archway School, Stroud) for 25 years and were heard by over 6,000 different young people. This also helped to fulfil the prophesy from Duncan White (page 99)

---

## FREE ALBUM DOWNLOAD
### Many of the songs mentioned in this book are available free of charge from:
www.poeticjustice4.bandcamp.com/releases

---

### *Inspired by God*
*I been thinking 'bout the good times,*
*been thinking 'bout the fun,*
*Been a wandering in the darkness*
*and a wondering what've I done?*
*(repeat)*
*Feeding off the memories but memories fade and die,*
*Doom and gloom and darkness over head*
*in an ever changing sky.*

*Chorus:*
*Inspiration come, inspiration go,*
309

*Exactly where it go, aint no body know.  x2*

*I hear the sound.... I hear the sound,*
*I hear the sound of the nightingale*
*as it sits away up high,*
*Unaware of darkness looming, looming in the sky.*
*Riders on the backs of horses running from the storm,*
*No inspiration's needed now*
*we must be home by dawn!*
*Yeshua Adonai we love you!*
*People, people, people, people everywhere,*
*Hurrying, scurrying without a care.*
*On their way to nowhere, walking in their sleep*
*People keep looking, people keep searching,*
*searching to stay alive.*
*People keep looking, people keep searching,*
*for that feeling good inside.*
*Are you searching for that feeling*
*that feels good inside?*
*Are you searching for that feeling*
*to make you stay alive?*
*Yo people!*
*What are you searching for?*
*Are you searching for inspiration?*
*Well I'll tell you.*
*When you find your inspiration*
*then take some good advice.*
*Are you inspired by good?*
*Are you inspired by bad?*
*Are you inspired by Jesus Christ?*
*God gave his Holy Spirit, inspiration to us all.*
*So don't give up, just ask yourself,*

310

*What's that inspiration for?*
*[Chorus]*

### *Reality*

*The dream generator keep on dreaming the dream.*

*Chorus:*
*Reality, reality, it happen to you and*
*it happen to me.*
*Reality, reality it happens to us all.  X2*

*The dream generator is the major dominator,*
*Influencing the way of life.*
*You gotta keep dreaming, dreaming a dream,*
*A big car or a beautiful wife.*
*Hey there mister average what is your dream?*
*Are you just another dreaming fool?*
*Do you gamble, do you bet,*
*are you a millionaire yet?*
*Do you dream about winning the pools?*
*Is there a pot of gold at the end of the rainbow?*
*A yellow brick road showing you which way to go?*
*Is there a pot of gold at the end of the rainbow?*
*A yellow brick road showing you which way to go?*

*[Chorus]*

*If you dream about loving,*
*then you dream about giving.*
*If you dream giving,*
*then you dream about living.*

311

*If you dream about living,*
*then you dream about lying*
*If you dream about lying,*
*then you dream about crying.*
*If you dream about crying*
*you dream about love!*

*Now reality happens to us all,*
*Just as pride comes before a fall.*
*Whether you dream or whether you don't.*
*Whether you will or whether you won't.*

*[Chorus]*

*Are you looking for a high, when you're feeling low,*
*Escape into a chemical and life begins to glow.*
*It's easy to say "yes", but you'd rather answer no.*
*You've tried all of the rest, but this high is the best,*
*So why is there an element of doubt?*
*I'll tell you now for why,*
*cuz when you're flying high,*
*You're the one that's really losing out!*

*[Chorus]*

*Are you a running and a hiding*
*from the things you have seen?*
*Hiding your face in a video screen.*
*Take a look at the dream in your head if you can,*
*The dream in your head's about a little man.*
*Are you a Mario or Sonic, Street Fighter Two,*
*Lost in a world where nothing is true?*

. *Are you a Mario or Sonic, Street Fighter Two,*
*Lost in a world where nothing is true?*
*Get real, stop dreaming a dream!*
*Get real, stop dreaming a dream!*
*Get real, stop dreaming a dream!*
*Get real and stop your dreaming!*

*Now there is the ultimate game,*
*With your helmet on it's inside your brain.*
*But the helmet of salvation,*
*Is the helmet of the nation.*
*Virtual reality or reality that's absolute,*
*The choice is yours,*
*put the helmet on and get to know the truth!*
*Get real you know what I'm saying!*
*Get real you know what I mean!*
*Get real you know what I'm praying!*
*Get real and stop your dreaming!*
*Get real you know what I'm saying!*
*Get real you know what I'm praying!*
*Get real you know what I'm saying!*
*Get real and stop your dreaming!*

### *Poetic Justice*
*Chorus:*
*If you could rap your way into Heaven.*
*If you could rap your way out of hell!*
*The whole world would be rapping,*
*The good the bad as well. [repeat]*

*You can't try to justify the things that you still do.*

313

*You might die, might even fry,*
*unless you find what's true*
*So I rap, let's rap, c'mon rap, let's rap, GO!*
*If you are a kid or you are a child,*
*Get poetic get justice get reconciled*
*You gotta get in the light get poetic.*
*If you follow the dark you're pathetic.*

*So I rap in time, I rap with rhyme,*
*but there's something I've gotta say,*
*I rap for good and I rap for God*
*cuz there's something I've gotta say*
*I rap for good and I rap for God*
*and I get down on my knees and pray.*
*When He speaks to me, it's shear poetry,*
*but words just can't explain.*
*The way that I feel, I know that God is real*
*so I rhyme in time again.*

*Though I've told you before I'll tell you again.*
*I'll tell you again and again and again.*
*I'll keep telling you just as long as it takes,*
*You to realise we all make mistakes.*
*Rapping is easy, but you know it's not the way.*
*You gotta pray to God in Heaven*
*and this is what you say.*
*Please forgive me God*
*for the things that I have done.*
*I believe in Jesus your one and only Son!*

*[Chorus]*

314

### The Word

*Baby craving, craving baby, craving to be fed,*
*Gotta keep craving, gotta keep feeding,*
*else you wind up dead!*
*Don't matter if you're rich, don't matter if your poor.*
*Starvation hits the nation and it happens to us all.*

*Chorus:*
*You gotta feed on the word.*
*You gotta feed on the word.*
*You gotta feed on the word of the Lord*
*You gotta feed on the word.*
*You gotta feed on the word.*
*You gotta feed on the word of my Lord God.*

*There's a feeling of hunger deep inside,*
*I don't wanna eat because of my pride.*
*But pride it comes before a fall,*
*That feeling of hunger happens to us all.*
*Satisfaction, satisfaction, never can get enough,*
*Of the right stuff, you know what I'm saying?*
*Nuff said I've said enough!*

*[Chorus]*

*If you wanna feed, you gotta have a read!*
*If you wanna feed, you gotta have a read!*
*If you wanna feed, you gotta have a read!*
*You gotta water the seed!*
*But don't get choked upon the weed!*
*Do you read or do you not?*
*You gotta water the seed when the sun is hot.*

315

*You gotta water the seed and let it grow.*
*You gotta water the seed and more seed sow!*

*Spiritual nourishment,*
*it's the word of God, there's no supplement.*
*If you feed the word, your spirit will grow,*
*Feed the spirit within and more seeds sow.*

*[Chorus]*

*If your feeding on the word,*
*you get closer to the Lord.*
*Check it out this word is living.*
*So take a look inside, get a new start to life,*
*From a God that is forgiving.*
*Can't judge a book by it's cover,*
*get into the word you'll discover.*
*There's a God in Heaven that you can call Dad,*
*With a Son that you can call Brother.*

*[Chorus]*

*Baby craving, craving baby, craving to be fed,*
*Gotta keep craving, gotta keep feeding,*
*else you wind up dead!*
*[repeat]*

### ***Keep on mocking***
*Chorus:*
*Hear you laughing, laughing at me,*
*Laughing with a heart of misery.*

316

*See you mocking, mocking what I do,*
*You mocking bless me don't you know it's true!*
*[repeat]*

*What d'you think your laughing at now?*
*Gonna let us in on the joke?*
*Are you laughing at me?  Are you laughing at him?*
*Are you laughing at some other bloke?*
*Everywhere I go, everything I do,*
*I hear the sound of laughter.*
*Faces smiling and fingers pointing*
*people heading for disaster.*
*Nothing wrong with having a laugh.*
*Nothing wrong with a bit of fun.*
*If no one in the world ever had a laugh,*
*No work would ever get done.*
*If you have a laugh it aint that bad.*
*All work and no play it make Jack bad.*
*If you have a laugh it aint that bad.*
*All work and no play it make Jack bad.*
*[Chorus]*

*Just wait a while before you smile*
*and ask the question "why?"*
*Do you laugh at my belly?*
*Do you laugh cuz I'm smelly?*
*Can you look me in the eye?*
*When I ask you do you know what's true?*
*Do you know what is a lie?*
*When I ask you are you laughing at me?*
*Are you laughing at the man in the sky?*

*[Chorus]*

*Are ya laughing by yourself?*
*Or ya laughing with your friends?*
*If ya laughing for a reason*
*keep on laughing to the end.*
*If ya laughing by yourself?*
*Or ya laughing with your friends?*
*If ya laughing for a reason*
*keep on laughing to the end.*
*If ya laughing cuz someone else does,*
*And you don't want to look out of place.*
*Just think again, what your laughing about,*
*About the look upon my face.*
*If you laugh at me because I'm free,*
*All I feel for you is sorry.*
*They laughed at the Boss*
*as they hung him on the cross,*
*All his thoughts for your tomorrow.*

*[Chorus]*

*Now this is nearly the end of this song,*
*Or the end of you if you wait too long.*
*Don't laugh at me anymore,*
*You can laugh with me, you know the score.*
*Don't have to be weak, like the rest of the sheep,*
*if you know what's true.*
*You can be blessed, just forget the rest,*
*And let them laugh at you.*

*Blessed are those who are persecuted in my name.  x4*

*Woe to you who laugh now,*
*For you will morn and weep.  x2*
*Blessed are those who are persecuted in my name.  x2*


### *Cross the line*
*Chorus:*
*There's no time to wait!*
*No more hesitate!*
*Think about it no more time,*
*Jump up step out and cross the line!*

*Check it out this life of ups and downs,*
*Of in and outs and merry-go-rounds.*
*A life of good, a life of bad,*
*A life of happy sad and mad!*
*Some people are crazy, some just lazy!*
*Work hard, play hard, live hard, die hard.*
*Filthy dirty, squeaky clean,*
*All questions and answers, you know what I mean.*

*[Chorus]*

*Black or white, short or tall,*
*Fat or thin, or large or small.*
*God loves you all.*
*God loves you all.*
*Summer, winter, rain or shine,*
*You gotta get on up and cross the line.*
*Get up a, get down.*

*Some things are happening, but some things aint,*

*Do you know what happens to all wet paint?*
*Starts off wet, but it ends up dry,*
*You gotta cross the line if you don't wanna die.*
*Now I'll explain to you the words of this song,*
*Some things are right, some things are wrong.*
*One hand is left, the other is right,*
*Work all day and sleep all night!*
*[Chorus]*

*Now the words of this song that I rap to you*
*is communication through and through.*
*You may not understand it,*
*but you know what to do,*
*Get rid of the false and follow the true.*
*The truth that I am talking about,*
*Is the kind of truth that leaves no doubt.*
*No doubt of what is in your mind,*
*Jump up step out and cross the line.*
*[Chorus]*

## Norman Warren's prayer
## referred to on page 90.

*Lord Jesus Christ, I know that I have sinned*
*in my thoughts words and actions.*
*There are so many good things I have not done.*
*There are so many sinful things I have done.*
*I am sorry for my sins and turn from everything*
*I know to be wrong.*
*You gave your life upon the cross for me.*
*Gratefully I give my life back to you.*
*Now I ask you to come into my life.*
*Come in as my Saviour to cleanse me.*
*Come in as my Lord to control me.*
*And I will serve and follow you all the*
*remaining years of my life.*
*Amen*

**Please review this book on Amazon and Goodreads – Thank you!**

**Brendan Conboy has an active MINISTRY for GOD**

**Brendan is looking forward to hearing from you**

*Contact Brendan at the following:*
*Email – bmconboy@gmail.com*
*Phone - +44 (0)1453 731008*
*Mobile – 07980 404873*
*www.brendanconboy.co.uk*

**The following pages contain information about Brendan's book titles (Bibliography).**

## The Golden Thread – Biography
### *A true story of fear, forgiveness and faith*
First published – 1$^{st}$ September 2015

Brendan Conboy grew up in fear and confusion, struggling with many personal issues. These experiences formed a foundation which could have ended in disaster, but instead, became the motivator to want to make a positive difference.

## Issues – Teen / YA Fiction
### *We all have issues… Can a bully change?*
First published – 23$^{rd}$ January 2019

Marcus Daniel was a caring, intelligent, larger than average ten year old. His parents changed and then so did he. Now Marcus is thirteen years old and a spiteful bully, full of anger, rage and pain. His actions have changed others. Will the fear, pain and rage win?

## My Foundation for Life – Semi Biog / Scriptural Teaching
*14 underpinning and impacting scriptures*
First published – 19<sup>th</sup> February 2019

What is it that makes some of us more resilient than others? I am sure that psychologists will have several long-winded explanations to answer this question, but I believe that we can increase our resilience by building our lives on a foundation of truth

## Rhyme Time – Poetry
*Poems with a message for you to read.*
*Poems of truth that plant a seed.*
First published – 13<sup>th</sup> November 2020

# The Invasion of the MIMICS
## Science Fiction / Dystopian / Fantasy
*They're already here... Invading your country...*
*Dwelling in your home... Living in your body!*
First published – 21st October 2020

Climate change had been predicted long ago, but not one person could foresee the events that had unfolded. Humanity is defeated, civilization lost, all hope has gone. Enlightenment is the new belief, but there are those that refuse to believe.

# The Land of Make Believe – Children's fantasy in rhyme
*Based on the story of doubting Thomas*
First published – 4th March 2021

Also scheduled for 2021:

The PSALMS in Rhyme

ONE GOD – Many Names!

The LEGACY of the MIMICS

Printed in Great Britain
by Amazon